MILTON'S PARADISE MISLAID

MILTON'S PARADISE MISLAID

Milton's PARADISE MISLAID

BILLY MILTON

JUPITER · LONDON

First published in 1976 by
JUPITER BOOKS (LONDON) LIMITED
167 Hermitage Road, London N4.

SBN 904041 67 0

Composed on the Monophoto in 11/13 pt Bembo 270
and originated by Servis Filmsetting Limited, Manchester.
Printed and bound in Great Britain by
R. J. Acford Limited, Chichester, Sussex.

Contents

Acknowledgements

Many people have helped and contributed to this volume of memories. I would particularly like to thank John Maxwell, David Drummond of 'Pleasures of the Past', Harry Stanley (an especial debt), Mander and Mitcheson, Stephen Watts, Clive Gay, James Tolleth, Lady Molly Daubeny, Con Mahoney, Graham Tomlinson and Tony Martin.

Special thanks are also due to David Lewin of the *Daily Mail* who, on 9 November 1966, gave me the spur to write *Paradise Mislaid*.

The verse on page 35 is from 'I Travel Alone', published in *Lyrics*, Copyright © Noël Coward, 1965, and is reproduced by kind permission of his Estate. The lyrics for 'I'm the Only Fakir on the Pier', 'Acknowledgements' and 'Fairy Blue Bell' are included here by courtesy of Michael Treford.

BILLY MILTON
Kensington, 1976.

vii

MILTON'S PARADISE MISLAID

CHAPTER ONE

Overture

My FATHER, HARRY MILTON, LOOKED LIKE A PERMANENT juvenile lead. He wore a neat grey bowler, hacking jacket and cravat, smart shoes and always had a clove carnation buttonhole. He was light-hearted, debonair, vain and generous to a fault.

Harry Milton of M. & W. Milton, 6 Park Lane, London, W.1., was a famous whip and jobmaster. He supplied Queen Victoria with carriage horses and riding hacks. King Edward VII and the Duke of Connaught would sit in our yard at No 6 and Father would show them some of the most beautiful horses in London. Sir John Cowans commandeered many of them for the 1914–18 war. Because of financial difficulties, the business at Park Lane and our Riding School in Shepherd Market were later sold. The former went to Lord Cowdray, and became the R.A.F. Club; the latter is now a block of flats.

Mother, *née* Hilda Jackson, daughter of Tom Jackson the famous cigar merchant of Panton Street, W.1., was on the stage – a chorus girl in *Floradora* at the Lyric Theatre. She had lovely dark hair, brown eyes, a tiny well-corseted waist, wore large-brimmed hats and skirts that swished most excitingly. Her nature was warm and loving and she had a wonderful sense of humour. Father's courtship was persistent. Every night he would drive to the theatre in his private hansom and take her out to supper. Despite strong opposition from many other stage-door johnnies, he eventually won her heart and hand in marriage.

My birth was a bitter disappointment to my parents who desperately wanted a girl: in fact they had a girl's name and clothes all ready. I believe that many of the problems I later faced emanated from the feeling that I wasn't wanted. A series of events when still a child left me with that recurring bad dream.

The first shock I experienced was when my parents gave away my beautiful green parrot. It usually sat on the handlebars of the tricycle I proudly rode along Howley Place, Paddington, where I was born on 8 December 1905. Apparently our parlourmaid had teased the bird and it bit her. The second was the disappointment of seeing Mother burn my collection of coloured bus tickets. She had been told they were liable to harbour germs. Then there was the whacking Father gave me with a hairbrush. Evidently he had called me several times and I hadn't answered; I didn't hear his call. Unfortunately the reasons for these punishments were never explained to me. I became nervous and uncertain and, whenever I couldn't hear anyone moving about the house, I would call out anxiously from the room I shared with my brother for assurance that my parents were still in the house. If they did not reply, because they were bored with answering my repeated calls, I'd panic – scared they had deserted me.

Harry, six years older, was a wonderful brother and I loved him dearly. He understood my fears, knew I was scared of the dark and made sure there was a nightlight in our room so I could sleep, unafraid.

One night a week I was allowed to stay up late to join the family for music in the drawing room. Mother played the piano and often accompanied Father singing his favourite melody, 'The Campbells Are Coming'. My great moment came when Mother left the piano and I ran forward to pound the keyboard with my small clenched fists, shouting 'Fireman's music!' These first performances at the piano must have indicated my future interest in the instrument.

Thomas Cook, founder of Cook's Tours (a delightful but eccentric man) was friendly with my father. The bond between them was the love of horses and his admiration for my mother. Our entire family would often stay with him at Sanowe Park, his Norfolk home. After a particularly heavy lunch one Sunday, he ordered his coach and four horses to be brought out and he drove us round his vast estate. During the drive he suddenly decided to take a short cut across what he thought was a shallow lake; but it wasn't. The coach stuck in the mud and the water all but drowned my mother, Harry and me who were trapped inside. Well

Family group. Notice my girlish clothes.

My father driving a four-in-hand at the Richmond Horse Show.

after 1.00 a.m., everyone was awakened by the fire alarm. Thomas Cook had pressed the bells connecting him with all the servants' quarters and his private Fire Brigade. He imagined the thatched roof of one of the cottages had caught fire and directed the firemen to turn their hoses on it. Back in London, I recall the family once again accompanied Thomas Cook on a wild escapade down Bond Street: this time he drove a coach and six horses. Wearing a pair of thick gloves, he scattered heated shilling pieces to the astonished pedestrians and laughed at their vain efforts to pick them up.

When my parents left me at Clare House, Margate, my first prep-school, I remember standing on the steps watching their carriage recede into the distance. Panic-stricken, I ran along the steep cliff-top until I fell exhausted. My only other memory of the school was that Mother, remembering my eagerness to thump the piano at home, arranged for me to take lessons from the music teacher. She was very strict. Mistakes or inattention brought a sharp rap across the knuckles with a long black ruler. I hated her and gave up the lessons but, whenever I could get into the music-room alone, I tinkled around on the piano and started to teach myself to play by ear. These setbacks began to give me the determination to do things my way.

My next school was Lancing College, situated on the Sussex Downs at Shoreham. The boys, most of them from rich families and rather snobbish, were carefully prepared to take their eventual place in society. They made fun of me when they discovered I was a horse-dealer's son. I ignored them because most of my days were spent dreaming of the theatre or designing posters for revues I was determined to produce. I learned practically nothing in the classroom and for this I got the cane. The procedure was that you bent over the bootbox in the changing-room. Two prefects watched for fair play and the third would run across the room and deliver a stroke with each run until your backside stung like a hornet's nest.

To make life more unpleasant, Tom Driberg, who later became a Member of Parliament, had me bullied. He didn't do the bullying himself but got two of his satellites to waylay me as I went to chapel. I decided to do something about it; I found a large medicine bottle labelled 'To be taken three times daily' and filled it with sherry which I had bribed one of the staff to buy me at the local pub. Then taking several large swigs, I sorted out my persecutor and shook the daylights out of him. After that I was left severely alone.

At Lancing Driberg seemed to regard himself as a Cardinal Richelieu figure; the other boys certainly did and he would do everything to encourage them. For instance, it was the custom on Sunday night for one side of the dormitory to visit the other, the purpose – mutual masturbation. It was considered bad form to express any reticence. I remember very clearly coming back from a cross-country run and saying 'I really am too tired' – to be greeted with the most horrendous silence and cold stares. With the moon peering through the windows, the sight and sound of eager hands exploring each other on gently rocking beds will always remain with me as an epitome of schoolboy togetherness. One was carried away by the excitement, and oblivious of anything else. But there was a figure that glided from one corner to another, seldom doing anything, just observing. This was Driberg. He got his satisfaction that way.

Driberg had great intelligence, a good deal of compassion, and could easily divorce the two. If he decided intellectually that he wanted something his emotions were turned off. Warmth of feeling was a luxury he allowed himself from time to time, but only when it could not possibly jeopardize the desires, ambitions and pretensions he had arrived at by way of pure cerebration. Whatever success he enjoyed was the result of this ability. Yes, he has championed many good causes, he has helped considerable numbers of distressed people, but he never possessed that warmth which characterizes the true mensch.

Over the years I often bumped into Driberg, usually in Soho, where he would be surrounded by hangers-on from the clubs he used to frequent. I would say, 'Oh my God! You've ruined my day!' – but not a flicker of emotion would cross his face. He was above everything he wanted to be above. Probably the only time life ever 'fingered' him was in the 1930s when he was 'William Hickey' of the *Daily Express*. I do not know the exact circumstances, but it was said that he was discovered during a police raid in a bed with two sailors. There was a tremendous uproar, and I was told that if Lord Beaverbrook had not interceded and prevented the case from coming to court Driberg would have been ruined. As it was he quietly left the *Express* some months later, was married (but it did not last long) and went to work for the old *Reynold's News* before standing for Parliament.

Whether Driberg took the active or passive role in homosexual encounters one will never know. The most aggressive and outgoing men are often passive in bed, while meek and unassuming types are active buggers between the sheets. Driberg may have varied his approach, but I am quite sure much of his pleasure was gained from the 'control' that comes from engaging an eager participant in a sexual scene.

I presume that Tom will have carried his secrets with him to the grave. It remains to be seen what will be revealed in the half-finished *Memoirs*....

At Lancing I started to compose songs and once again took piano lessons. One day in the practice room the music master came in. 'What on earth are you playing?' he demanded. 'Something by Noël Coward, sir' I replied. 'Noël who?' Then after a thoughtful pause he said 'Oh yes, that's the fellow who writes music with his tongue in someone else's cheek.'

My housemaster tried to mould me into the manageable pattern of boys who did everything they were told; I felt he wanted to crush my spirit. One summer afternoon I was told to report to him at the meadow where he was shooting rooks. As I approached he had just shot a bird and it lay fluttering on the ground. He ordered me to bang its head against the tree trunk. The idea was repellent and my attempt futile. Seeing the bird still alive he ground its head into the earth with his heel. He then looked at me to see what impression this had made; I was nauseated.

He demonstrated his desire to break my spirit on another occasion. There had been trouble in the dormitory when I and some of the boys had been caught masturbating. Others were involved but they would not own up, so he decided to beat everyone. The usual time for punishment was either the morning or evening. I was told to go to his study in the afternoon. Everybody else was out playing cricket. After the beating he extended his hand as if he expected me to shake it; the look I gave him registered what I felt. Anyway his campaign to stifle my spirit had the reverse effect on me and stimulated still further my determination to become an individualist.

During school holidays Mother encouraged me in the appreciation of music of all kinds. She knew the piano was a source of comfort to me whenever things went wrong. Sometimes I would even practise in the dark. My grandfather had the misfortune to go blind and I wanted to make sure that if I ever lost my sight I would still be able to play

Apart from the usual schoolboy crushes at college, my first emotional friendships which must not be confused with love, my first real sex-thrill in the opposite direction was provided by an incident at a cinema during the 'hols'. I experienced an exquisite torture when the glamorous film star, dressed in a tight-fitting, black satin gown, turned to the camera and walked towards it. As her beautiful bra-less breasts slowly undulated I came to life with a bang! It happened again years later in New York. I was walking down Fifth Avenue on my way to play the matinee at the Selwyn Theatre when I became aware of a young girl in front of me wearing black satin. The wobbling of her cute little bottom so frustrated me I forgot the time and followed doggedly. But when I discovered how late it was, I ran all the way to the theatre. I called this my 'black-satin period'.

At sixteen, I took my first and only singing lesson. I was recommended to a teacher who had been, in her time, an awesome Brunhilde and shaken the foundations of many an Opera House with her powerful vibrato. Now, at an uncertain age, she was still explosive, expansive and expensive. Her lesson left me absolutely exhausted. She commanded me to place both hands on her melonesque bosom and gaze down her cavernous throat so that she could demonstrate her breathing technique. Then, without any warning, she emitted a shattering note that sounded just like a liner leaving harbour. I decided there and then that my simple scales that I practised at home would be more useful. Fortunately my parents agreed!

Brother Harry had grown into a tall, handsome young man and I tried to emulate everything he did. Once I hid behind our big red leather sofa in the drawing room which I knew he and his young lady used for love-making after lunch on Sundays when the coast was clear. They had no idea I was there as I never made a sound during their amorous entanglements. The annoying part was that I could not see anything.

My interest in the opposite sex was now increasing and I was pleased to get an invitation to the seventeenth birthday party of Betty Harris. She was one of a family of sisters, Dinah, Peggy and Jill, who ran a dancing school. As I sat like a wall-flower, Betty said 'When are you going to ask me to dance?' 'I can't dance' I replied. 'Don't be silly' she said dragging me to my feet. The first steps proved my point. 'Oh dear' she said and with determination insisted 'Be here tomorrow at ten o'clock, I'll teach you'.

Directly I had mastered the fox-trot, waltz and tango, I was away like a bird; I couldn't stop dancing, day in, day out. Whenever my parents went out, up would come the rugs on the parquet floor in the drawing room and I would whirl, leap, turn cartwheels and pirouette to the tune 'I'm Just Wild about Harry'.

It became obvious to my father I was not happy at Lancing College so he took me away. He knew a director of Selfridges, and thus I was to become an underpaid, overworked shop-assistant at the famous store in London's Oxford Street. My salary was 18/6d a week, clocking on at 8.45 a.m., and working from 9.00 until 6.00 p.m., in the 'Gentleman's

Riding with my father and brother Harry in Hyde Park. My father often used to show off his horses there, as he could be sure of a large gathering of affluent society.

Outfitting Department'. My store-name was 'Mr Shoreham'.

Gordon Selfridge, a tall white headed American, usually wore a top-hat when he walked through the store at least once a day. He was keen on employing young men straight from public school or university. My Oxford Street companions included Count Anthony de Bosdari (later founder of Brunswick Records) and the Vicomte de Sibour (who married one of the Selfridge family).

Two things stand out in my memory of Selfridges. First was the generosity of Gordon Selfridge when he settled the enormous gambling debts incurred by his beloved Dolly Sisters, the American dancers who captivated London and Paris with their Pony Dance. His largesse landed him in financial difficulties. My second memory was the order I took from the Honourable Mrs Lionel Harris – a birthday present for the then Prince of Wales (later Edward VIII) – a pair of white moiré silk braces to which she pinned a tiny design in diamonds of the Prince of Wales feathers, which expressed her love and devotion.

The work was uncreative and I could have strangled the customers who turned the stock upside down and left without buying a thing. Often when a customer approached me with the obvious intention to buy, I was pushed aside by older assistants eager to grab the commission.

Father insisted I dress in lounge suit instead of the regulation black coat and striped trousers, and wear a red carnation in my buttonhole. He said 'You will either get the sack or be promoted'. He was right, I was promoted. Eric Dunstan, who was Gordon Selfridge's private secretary, noticed my non-conformist attire and it led to my transfer to the publicity department. My salary was raised to 22/6d a week.

Some years later Eric Dunstan retired and we met again at his villa in Antibes when he gave a lunch for Somerset Maugham. There were twelve of us at the table. One of the guests, an elderly duchess, dropped off to sleep in the sultry atmosphere and spilled spaghetti bolognese down her dress. She awoke with a snort, her double chins snapped back into place. She looked round sheepishly. 'Oh dear' she said. 'I must have nodded off.' Eric came to her rescue: 'Don't worry, dear, anything you eat looks good on you'.

Somerset Maugham, who resembled an elderly turtle, sat next to me and we conversed sketchily during the meal. He looked frail and was obviously absentminded. Towards coffee-time he turned to me and stuttering badly, enquired 'What's happened to Eric Dunstan?' It was eerie, for there, sitting at the head of the table, was our host Eric Dunstan.

My duties in the Selfridges publicity department were to study lay-outs, inspect window displays and report on their presentation. The knowledge and experience I gained there was in later years to prove invaluable. The work brought me in touch with an American lady employed by the store as a fashion designer. Tall, blonde and beautiful, she soon became the partner in my first romance. We also shared another love, ballroom dancing. Every week we went to the Queen's Hall Roof, the popular *thé dansant* rendezvous above the famous concert hall in Langham Place. We danced every dance, a rather odd-looking couple, for she was much taller than me. My head just about came up to her ample bosom, in which it could nestle comfortably when the hall darkened for a waltz. The admission fee of five shillings included a set tea. As she had a healthy appetite and a great love for pastries, I was constantly worried in case she wanted more than was included in the price.

When I asked the publicity manager about a rise in salary he told me it wasn't possible. I said it might cause me to give up the job and try the theatre. His insulting reply, 'That's a pimp's profession', made me so angry I gave him notice immediately.

Father was ambitious for me in another direction and, before allowing me to try the theatre, he arranged an apprenticeship with Captain Ronald Fox, wine merchant of Crutched Friars in the City of London. I would live in France and learn the champagne trade.

For the princely sum of £4.10.0 a week, I worked at Maison Lanson Père et Fils in Reims. £3 a week for my keep and 30/- as pocket money. Once a month I was able to spend the weekend in Paris. Short of cash, I was forced to walk everywhere and soon I knew that beautiful city like the back of my hand. Most of the money was spent on entrance to the promenoirs of the Casino de Paris and Folies Bergère. Other times it was a gay night at 23 Rue Blondel, where the waitresses wore only tiny see-through lace aprons. Never in my wildest dreams did I think that one day I would appear at the Casino de Paris with one of the greatest stars in France.

Victor Lanson was my mentor and guide. When I wasn't out in the fields picking grapes, I was in the cellars at 7.30 in the morning. The patois I learned from the cellar-men proved invaluable when later I worked on the Paris stage. Most Englishmen find the *tu* and *ouille* sounds very difficult to pronounce in French, so they made me repeat over and over again *Tu le tutu chapeau pointu* and also *Chatouille mes couilles avec le fenouil*. Little did I know that roughly translated it was 'Tickle my balls with fennel'.

Harry, my brother, in his Royal Flying Corps uniform in front of his plane.

Arrangements were made for me to visit Dijon to meet some of Victor Lanson's friends who marketed burgundy in association with his firm. They were a charming family, but at that time were having quite a problem with the eldest son. He had found his feet with the ladies and was fast becoming the menace of the neighbourhood. The father suggested his son and I should go to Lyons to let off steam together.

Despite my romance in London with the American girl, it had left me technically still a virgin and my sexual education could certainly be improved by further experience. But I shall never forget the qualms I felt at the sight of the two 'ladies' we met in a restaurant where we dined; they were brassy-looking and not young. We were both seventeen and, drinking freely of champagne and burgundy, we soon got tight. The two *papillons de nuit* took us to a small hotel where we rented an apartment with bedroom and anteroom. My host (*he* was paying all the expenses) had first pick and chose the short, smiling and shifty one, leaving me with the one that was long, lanky and lascivious-looking. He also claimed the bedroom, leaving me the sparsely-furnished room with table, chair, screen and a sofa on which I was to receive my first real lesson in the art of making love.

I was so shy I asked my lady of the evening to retire behind the screen while I readied myself for action. She laughed at my request which together with the fact that I had had far too much to drink, tended to put me off. When I gave her the signal she emerged coquettishly, fluttering like a wounded butterfly. But encouraged by her expert ministrations I soon got into my stride and continued merrily until she complained '*J'ai des crampes dans mes cuisses. Tu ne jouis pas?*' ('I've cramp in my thighs. Aren't you coming yet?') I disregarded her remarks and continued on my course until panting and perspiring I triumphantly passed the winning post.

But as Noël Coward once said 'Every good deed has to be paid for', and a few days later when I had returned to Reims, I discovered that the lady had left me with a painful souvenir.

I found a new friend, Pierre Heidsieck, the son of Charles Heidsieck of the rival champagne firm. He enrolled me as a member of the exclusive 'Sporting Club' where I played tennis with Count Maxence de Polignac of Maison G. H. Mumm (he later gained notoriety during the Second World War because of his friendship with the Nazi diplomat, Count Ribbentrop) and swam in the club pool with Madame Emile Charbonneau, wife of the Mayor of Reims. What fascinated me was the way she managed to keep her heavily made up face from getting splashed.

My letters home became so infrequent my anxious parents asked a friend to contact me and ascertain how I was getting on. He was a middle-aged American. Trying to impress him I suggested a visit to the Palais Oriental, a newly-opened luxury brothel where special suites were available. They even had private garages for your car. He demurred, but I finally persuaded him.

When we arrived the madame was out so we settled down to drink champagne with two of the girls. When Madame eventually returned, the sight of my American friend brought a cry of delight. She remembered him as one of her best clients when, as a young man living in New York, he was a frequent visitor to the 'house' which she then ran on Central Park West. Madame summoned all her girls and instructed them that they were each to give us a touch of the 'deep throat' therapy and as a *coup d'estime*, Madame herself delivered the last *blow*.

On my return to London, Captain Fox decided I should become a commercial traveller. He said that would 'calm me down'. His original promise to me had been a substantial increase in salary and a base in London. I was most unhappy at this turn of events and demanded to know whether he intended to keep his original promise. When he said 'No', I gave him notice.

It was a bold step and in some ways I was sorry, because I had really enjoyed my association with the champagne trade and the many friends I had made. But it was now or never.

CHAPTER TWO

Beginners

I DINED THAT NIGHT WITH A GOOD FRIEND, THE HONOURABLE
Mrs Christabel Russell. She advised me to give an audition at Chez Henri
Club in Long Acre. She said she would organise the whole thing and also
take along a large party of friends to give me strong support.

Hastily I put an act together: songs, piano solo and finishing with a
dance. To my delight the audition was a success and resulted in my first
professional engagement. Salary ten pounds a week. The Houston Sisters
(Renée and Billie) were the stars of the Chez Henri cabaret and I appeared
each morning at 1.00. Both acts were accompanied by the house band,
Charlie Kunz and His Orchestra.

After that events moved quickly. For the next four years I worked non-
stop. Cabaret engagements included Ciro's, the Carlton Hotel, the Café
de Paris, the Kit Kat Club and the Embassy Club in Bond Street (the
playground of royalty).

Simultaneously I broke into films; initially as a guinea-a-day extra.
One day my friend Tom Helmore read in the *Evening News* that the great
Hollywood film director, Cecil B. de Mille, was looking for English
actors for his next epic. He was staying at the Carlton Hotel, Haymarket.
Though Tom and I had done nothing worth while up to that time, this
was a chance to get to Hollywood that two ambitious young actors
simply couldn't miss. I knew we could never get to see him without an

My first professional photograph.

appointment, so full of confidence we marched up to the receptionist and said 'We are reporters from the *Evening News* and wish to see Mr Cecil B. de Mille'. It worked! She telephoned and then said 'Will you gentlemen go to the first floor, where you will be met at the lift'. We were conducted to the ante-room by his secretary and asked to wait. With each passing minute we grew more nervous and apprehensive. The secretary finally ushered us in to face the great man. He was seated at an expansive desk, dressed in a white open-neck shirt (it was summer) ostensibly writing an endless letter. When eventually he looked up, he said nothing but scrutinised us very carefully. Then he rose slowly and as he came round the desk we noticed he was wearing his famous riding breeches and boots. He smiled thinly and said 'You are not reporters, you are actors!' Hollywood had to wait.

I landed a part in *London* with Hollywood star Dorothy Gish and Paul Whiteman and His Orchestra. Next I played a midshipman in *The Flag Lieutenant* with Henry Edwards and Chrissie White. I was so full of enthusiasm that in one scene, after landing my men from a destroyer, I led them up a cliff brandishing my sword, and disappeared into a large hole I hadn't seen! Following that came a part in *The Lodger* with Ivor Novello, the first suspense film directed by Alfred Hitchcock.

My star was also ascending in the theatre. First I got a part in the musical *Just a Kiss* at the Shaftesbury Theatre. I also understudied the star, Barrie Oliver, an American who taught the Prince of Wales to play the ukelele and to dance the new sensation, the Charleston.

One hot summer afternoon I was passing the courtyard that leads to the stage-door of the London Palladium. Taking the air was a perfect specimen of manhood. Wearing a short white and gold tunic and breastplate, his magnificent brawny, brown body made him look to me like a Greek God. I was transfixed and willingly answered his call to have a chat, sitting with him on a prop basket. I told him a few things about myself and learned he was the principal dancer of the Marian Morgan Dancers from America. This meeting led to many experiments in the sexual sphere that could parallel Noël Coward's *Private Lives*. He and his wife opened the door to a tumult of love-making and encouraged me to explore the many facets of sex: the one great gift nature has bestowed on all of us. They believed that the lack of courage to explore love-variations, caused the failure of many marriages. Their antidote was the threesome, or 'Chelsea sandwich', and I subsequently learnt that I was just one of many to have come between them.

This man much preferred these threesomes with his wife to be with another man. Another woman was not nearly so exciting. I have often met men with this inclination and I have always interpreted it as a sign of latent homosexuality. Similarly with husbands who do not mind their wives sleeping around – *as long as they tell them everything*, right down to the last detail. By behaving in this way, they tell themselves, they are not homosexuals. How could they be? They have never touched another man in their life!

White Birds Revue at His Majesty's Theatre came next. The cast was huge – Maurice Chevalier, Yvonne Valle, Jose Collins (of *Maid of the Mountains* fame), Anton Dolin and Ninette de Valois – to mention but a few. Lew Leslie, the American producer, had been successful in his hand-ling of coloured performers in his revue *Blackbirds* at the London Pavilion, but he wasn't so fortunate with white artists. His arrogance made him enemies and his lethargic disregard for detail was directly responsible for the failure of *White Birds*. It was a monumental flop and its backer, Everard Gates, lost a fortune. The show was top-heavy with stars and over-loaded with material. During rehearsals Leslie worked the cast and staff like galley-slaves. The pressure was so great one of the stage-hands (a newly-wed) cracked under the strain. When we arrived for rehearsal one morning, we saw the poor fellow dangling from a rope above the stage: he had hanged himself.

Lew Leslie had a violent row with French actress Lucienne Herval. He ordered her to be cut from the show. But she understood her contract (right down to the small print). Each night she made-up and dressed ready to go on stage. This entitled her to draw full salary although she never performed.

Jose Collins came back to rehearsal one day after a heavy lunch, in a belligerent mood. My partner, Doreen Reed, and I were running through a speciality dance for the Spanish scene in which Jose sang. Our entrance was to be made from a large tambourine. When Jose came on stage she shouted to Lew Leslie sitting in the stalls, 'I don't want any bloody dancers coming out of that fucking tambourine'. Needless to say, she had her way and our dance was cut.

Deeply shocked and hurt I went to sit at the back of the stage box and in the darkness shed tears of frustration. Suddenly I felt I was not alone. An arm encircled my shoulders and a kindly voice said 'You must expect things like this'. It was the principal male dancer. I had always thought him tough and a trifle grand, but this was the beginning of a life-long

Tom Hellmore, Billy Milton, Forrester Harvey and Humberston Wright as seen in *The Flag Lieutenant*, my second film.

News of the World impressions of *White Birds*.

friendship. We became intimate friends, and the next day a gold cigarette-case arrived from Asprey, the Bond Street jewellers. This was my consolation-prize from him. It was greatly admired by my parents and borrowed on numerous occasions whenever my brother wanted to impress a girl friend.

We drove to Oxford one weekend to attend a Fancy Dress Ball. We stayed at the Randolph Hotel where another friend, the Hon. Evan Morgan (the late Lord Tredegar) was also in residence. On the Sunday morning Evan phoned to invite us both to his suite for a preview of the costume he intended to wear that night. It was late breakfast-time when I knocked at his door. On opening it, there was his Lordship standing before the window stark naked except for a tiny wisp of grey-oyster tulle covering his 'Brighton rock'. I presumed he was illustrating his family motto 'Ready to Serve'.

White Birds started twenty minutes late on opening night. The delay was caused by Lew Leslie who had dropped one of his diamond dress-studs. He went berserk and held the curtain until it was found. By 11 00 that night we had just finished the *first* half of the revue and were shuddering at the thought of the second half because there had been no proper run-through. Standing in the prompt corner, Leslie tried frantically to re-arrange the running-order. This resulted in chaos. For example, the orchestra played a dance number when it should have been a sketch and the chorus girls started to dress for a scene which, unbeknown to them, had been cut. When the finale mercifully arrived the whole company was incorrectly dressed. Nobody had any idea of what was happening. It would have been laughable if it hadn't been so tragic. Such a waste of great talent *and* good money!

Maurice Chevalier had been wise. Before he and Yvonne Valle left France, he insisted that every penny of the three months guaranteed salary was to be paid into his Paris bank.

Following the closure of the show, Laddie Cliff, the impresario, asked me to appear in *Shake Your Feet* at the London Hippodrome, with Jack Hylton and His Band, Billy Merson, Milton Hayes and Joyce Barbour. It was a good show for me because I had five numbers to sing, including the big international hit 'Lucky Day'. In the show were sixteen young American beauties called The Gertrude Hoffman Girls. Their act was similar to the Esther Williams film *Water Ballet*, only they performed on long strips of suspended webbing. The ageing raconteur Milton Hayes, who was said to depend on a pair of bellows to take a deep breath, read

A review with sketches of *The Bow-Wows* from *Eve*.

amusing topical snippets from a newspaper. He had a thirty-minute break after his act which he devoted entirely to trying to persuade one of the Hoffman beauties to have sex with him. It was like trying to catch a butterfly with too small a net. He met with little success, until one day one butterfly was either too green or too slow and he did score a bullseye during an uncomfortable twenty-minute ride in a taxi.

Bow Wows at the Prince of Wales Theatre came next, with Davy Burnaby, Betty Chester, George Metaxa, Leonard Henry, Vera Bryer and Eddie Morris. It was really the *Co-Optimists* retitled. I took over from the famous American piano artist, Melville Gideon. The diminutive American-Canadian comedian, Eddie Morris, tried desperately hard to convert me to Christian Science. He brought me several books by Mary Baker Eddy to read, but when I came to the theatre after a New Year's Party with a giant hangover, he assured me it was a figment of my imagination. It was then I knew, it wasn't for me!

Subsequently I went into *Will O' the Whispers* at the Shaftesbury Theatre with the American recording star 'Whispering' Jack Smith (popular songs-at-the-piano act), heart-throb singer George Metaxa and comedian Billy Bennett. My conscience is pricked every time 'Whispering' Smith is mentioned. I was juvenile lead as well as being his understudy. There was a period when I caught a cold and also had a touch of tonsilitis. It didn't stop me from working, but it gave me an idea. I managed to get close to Jack and breathed heavily in his direction hoping he would catch my cold, lose his 'will-o'-the-whisper' voice and I would be able to play for him. In retrospect, I'm glad to say it didn't work!

During the daytime I made gramophone records under three different names for three different companies: His Masters Voice, Columbia and Piccadilly. I also sang vocals on recording sessions for Carroll Gibbons, Van Phillips and other famous dance orchestras. With Clifford Seyler (brother of actress Athene Seyler) I wrote revues for the B.B.C. Two of them, 'Djinn and Bitters' and 'Fancy Meeting You', featured the new radio comedian John Tilley and helped him on his road to fame.

My brother Harry was also doing well, playing juvenile lead with Gracie Fields in Archie Pitt's music hall revue *The Show's the Thing*. One night he announced to me that he was going to marry film actress Dorothy (Chili) Bouchier. This news astounded me as I had heard on the film-studio grapevine that she was *very* attached to her agent, Max Rocher. In fact, it was said that not long before the wedding, they had been on holiday together. For Harry's sake I decided to say nothing rather than chance destroying his happiness. It was a registry-office wedding, a quiet affair with just the two families present and Gracie Fields with her husband Archie Pitt. Every time I met Gracie after that, she always asked 'When are you going to get married, Billy?' Years later at the London Palladium where she was topping the bill, I went to her dressing-room and almost the first thing she asked was 'Are you married yet, luv?' Just to please her I replied 'Yes I am. The wife and four children are in Bournemouth.' At last Gracie was satisfied. She said contentedly, 'Marriage is luverly, isn't it luv?' I thought to myself, she should know – Archie Pitt, Monty Banks and Boris!

Harry's marriage ran smoothly until he partnered Jessie Matthews in *Hold My Hand* at the Gaiety Theatre. He and Jessie provided the love interest in the show, but Harry pursued Jessie off-stage as relentlessly as he did on-stage. The matrimonial mix-up between Harry Milton, Chili Bouchier, Sonnie Hale, Jessie Matthews and Evelyn Laye, received a good deal of publicity in the national press. Less publicised was the tragic result of the affair for my brother. Undoubtedly his conduct was reprehensible, but he got a tougher deal than he should have done.

Jessie's husband, Sonnie Hale, it was alleged, caused a meeting to be called of the West End Managers Association and they decided to blackball Harry. This decision resulted in my brother finding it increasingly difficult to get work in the theatre. Jessie had become a valuable asset as a star of stage and screen; her backers felt the need to protect their investment by forbidding them to meet. Some of the parties concerned have published their version of Harry Milton's affairs and what happened to him. His death prevented him answering back so, in fairness to my brother, I'll do it for him.

If it gives some satisfaction to any of those people who gently crucified my brother, he managed to find employment as assistant manager at the Brixton Empress Theatre, where he was very popular with management, artists and patrons. I played there on a Dorothy Squires variety bill. Harry never spoke of the past and was full of fun. When the Empress closed, Harry, though suffering from cancer of the larynx, continued working right to the end, in the packing department of John Barkers in High Street, Kensington.

The madness of love makes us do many strange things. Yes, the newspaper reports were true; Harry did fly an aeroplane over Jessie Matthews' house at Old Hampton several times, and each time he dropped a matchbox containing a single raspberry. He was foolish, but I think it's about

A publicity shot of my brother, Harry Milton.

[25]

News of the World impressions of *Will O' the Whispers*.

time he was left in peace.

Chili and I met briefly in the street at Bangor, North Wales, during the last war. We were there to broadcast for the B.B.C. Woefully she said 'Love has been so unkind to me', making herself the injured party. But on reflection I thought, Didn't Max Rocher the agent, Teddy Joyce the bandleader, Bluey Hill, and others offer homage at her shrine? Maybe it is a case of *Qui s'excuse, s'accuse*.

But to continue with my story. Up to this time I had been living with my parents, but felt that the moment had come for me to make a break, so I moved into a studio flat in Yeomans Row off Brompton Road, an area popular with people prominent in theatrical and artistic circles. My next door neighbour was painter-designer Oliver Messel (Lord Snowdon's uncle). He was a frequent visitor to my studio and I to his. This developed into an intense attachment which lasted until finally I had to leave for America.

I enjoyed throwing parties. The *Daily Mail* commented, 'The informal cabaret at Billy Milton's party last night was as full of stars as a Cochran revue. In succession we were entertained by Douglas Byng, Ivy St. Helier, Rex Evans, Peggy Wood, Billy Mayerl and Ursula Jeans. Gracie Fields sang the score of *Bitter Sweet* beautifully. I felt she could have played the leading role of Sarah if Noël Coward could have had a guarantee she wouldn't fool around in the part.'

I had previously taken six of my compositions to Gracie Fields' sumptuous home on Hampstead Heath. I expected to play them for her. Instead she said 'Leave them on the piano, luv. I'll go through them later.' My heart sank. I'd paid quite a lot to have them put on paper expertly, a job I cannot do myself. I also thought she might forget them as she was bombarded daily with songs sent to her by publishers.

Months later I was walking down Charing Cross Road and met a friend. He said, 'I like the way Gracie recorded your song "I've Got a Man"'. We were near Francis, Day & Hunter's music shop so I went in to hear the record. I was delighted that she hadn't forgotten my song after all.

For my birthday, the Rance of Pudakota entertained at her house in Chesterfield Street, Mayfair. *The Tatler* reported 'The drawing room was crowded with celebrities. Cathleen Nesbitt chatted with Lord Ava and his fiancee Maureen Guinness. Captain Scott-Robson and several other brilliant young men from the Foreign Office were nearby. Cecil Beaton, wearing an off-white suit, draped himself in the doorway. Felix Doubleday, banker son of the head of the American publishers Doubleday, Doran, talked about the Wall Street crash and its effect on the London Stock Exchange.' It was a period of slump, but I was one of the luckier people. My world looked bright and the future looked promising. The champagne flowed freely and among these people it seemed as if there was nothing wrong in the world: their world.

Mollie Pudakota loved parties, especially those given at Oxford. The particular party I recall took place on the first-floor of a house with a winding staircase. It was so crowded that people who wanted to get in or out of the small room had to push hard to do so. Mollie was leaning against the balustrade talking vivaciously to a handsome young under-graduate, when I and four other chaps wanted to get out. We heaved and shoved until finally we burst out and in so doing knocked Mollie flying over the balcony. She plummeted down like a sea-gull diving for fish and landed neatly in a big bowl of fruit salad on the trestle-table below. Thank heavens she was wearing her mink coat! It saved her from serious injury. Dripping with fruit juice, she furiously took off for London in her Rolls Royce.

Among the guests was a hearty bore. Someone stupidly put strong sleeping tablets in his glass of wine, in the hope it would pass him out of circulation for the rest of the night. Unfortunately, I picked up the glass by mistake, drank the potion meant for him and passed out. I awoke the next morning cold and nude on a single bed, surrounded by four candles, with two lilies across my chest and a third stuck up my fundamental orifice.

It was Frankie Leverson's invitation to drinks at his studio in Geralds Row that was to change the whole course of my life. Frankie, a dapper little Dane, danced with his partner June (later Lady Inverclyde) in cabaret at the Embassy Club in Bond Street. After a few martinis, Frankie showed me over the studio. In the middle of the large room was a raised dais on which stood a Steinway piano. There was a Romeo and Juliet balcony, and we carried the amorous Shakespearian scene into his large and friendly bedroom. When it was time to leave, he explained that he was spending the weekend with Noël Coward and would put in a word for me with Noël about his new revue. I'd heard that sort of promise before, but it was kind of him and I said so.

Just as I was leaving he said, 'Why don't you wait a few minutes and meet the Rocky Twins, two of the most handsome young men you'll ever see. Then if you are free, we can go out to dine somewhere.' It was

Billy Bennett and I in a sketch from *Will O' the Whispers*.

A Little Light Refreshment with a Dash of Fancy
Book by CLIFFORD SEYLER
Music by BILLY MILTON and HARRY PEPPER

The Persons :

Jimmy Bitson (commonly known as ' Bitters ')
HORACE PERCIVAL
Amelier Victorier 'Opkins (vulgarly known as ' Squibs ')
ANONA WINN
Mrs. 'Opkins........⎫ Parents of the ⎫ MAY KENNETH
Albert 'Ennery Bitson⎰ above respectively⎰ CLIFFORD SEYLER
Paul Winthrop (a rich collector of curios) ......IVAN FIRTH
The Unknown Lady...................DOROTHY SULLIVAN
The Djinn .... VICTOR LEWISSOHN
A Policeman, a Kitten, an Organ-grinder, Villagers, Natives, etc.

The Scenes :

1. A London Street
2. In a Motor Car
3. A Private Museum
4. A Dip in the Sea
5. Cairo—The Market Place
6. The Desert
7. Vauxhall Gardens Long Ago
8. A Hundred Years from Now
9. Somewhere in Summerset
10. Same as Scene 1

Pianos : PATRICIA ROSSBOROUGH and HARRY PEPPER
THE REVUE CHORUS

Programme for 'Djinn and Bitters', one of my revues for the B.B.C.

[30]

just as Frankie had said; they were unbelievably handsome and so alike you couldn't tell which was which. As one hostess remarked, you could never be sure which one you were talking to, or had gone to bed with. Years later I met them in Paris where they had become a sensation at the Casino de Paris with the Dolly Sisters – you could hardly tell the Dollys from the Rockys.

Frankie Leverson did speak to Noël about me and it resulted in my having two auditions at the London Pavilion, one for Charles B. Cochran and the other for Noël himself. I was offered second juvenile lead in the Cochran revue *This Year of Grace* which Noël had written and was going to co-star in with Beatrice Lillie at the Selwyn Theatre on Broadway. I was also to understudy The Master, the salary was fifty pounds a week, and if I played for him, eighty.

Before the show went into rehearsal, Noël fell ill and so did I. He had an operation for piles and I caught diphtheria. I cursed my bad luck. It was a race against time who would get well first. Even before I was declared free from infection I wrote to Cochran to tell him that I would definitely be in his office just before rehearsals were due to start. My doctors warned me seriously against going to America without first taking a long holiday, but I was determined to go.

With Mother's help I made a shaky and uncomfortable journey to Margate for a week's rest. Diphtheria is very debilitating and I slowly regained a little of my strength. But supported by a walking stick and fortified by a couple of glasses of port wine to restore colour to my cheeks, I presented myself, as promised, at Mr Cochran's office in Bond Street. The great man looked at me aghast as I was so pallid and thin. He said that hearing of my illness he had given my part to another artist. I was so distressed I broke down and wept. Seeing my unhappiness he relented and I was re-instated.

CHAPTER THREE

Broadway with Noël Coward

T HE *This Year of Grace* COMPANY SAILED FOR NEW YORK ON THE *S.S. President Harding*; the crossing was very rough. Noël and Beatrice Lillie had gone on ahead, each on a separate liner. Doing it this way meant that there were *two* big press receptions.

Besides Noël and Bea, the cast included Florence Desmond, Oriel Ross (later Lady Poulett), Audrey Pointing (later Lady Doverdale) and the dancers Marjorie Moss and George Fontana. We made our way by train to Baltimore where we were to open. I stayed at Kernan's, a hotel adjacent to the theatre and popular with theatrical folk.

One morning the phone rang. A man's voice said 'You won't know me but I am a friend of Roy Royston'. Roy was a friend of mine who had played America several times, so I asked this chap up to my room. He said his brother, a famous jockey, was riding that afternoon and had given him some valuable inside information. I am not a betting man, except for an occasional flutter on the Derby and Grand National, but this fellow sounded convincing so I gave him the money to place some bets. During the matinée he came to my dressing room and told me excitedly I had won and so had several other members of the company, including Beatrice Lillie. He said he would collect our winnings and bring them to the theatre after the matinée. In the meantime he said he had two more 'certainties' and if I gave him more stake money he would bet on these horses and I would finish the day showing a large profit. When I suggested he use my previous winnings as stake money, he became evasive. We never saw him again, but I remembered his face and reported the matter to the police; they caught him shortly afterwards.

Our reception at Baltimore was lukewarm, but when we opened at the Selwyn Theatre in New York, it was ecstatic. Bea twisted the audience round her little finger. It seemed to me that Noël found the applause for her first entrance embarrassingly lengthy. *Variety*, the American show-business newspaper with an international reputation, reported '*This Year of Grace*, a super personality revue. Smash hit with wit and polish.'

Noël's relations with the New York press were sometimes high-handed. The influential *New York Daily Mirror* sent a man to take photographs of Noël and Bea for a pictorial series they were running. Noël thought it was cheap publicity and said he didn't want any part of it. Next day they commented 'Mr Coward, smelling slightly of Chanel and waving his platinum bracelet in our faces, said he didn't want publicity in our news-paper. Here are a few of those who do.' Then followed a list of over four hundred famous theatrical names. It was a break for me because I posed with Bea for the pictures.

When the show was well under way and running smoothly, I started composing new songs. After the audience had gone, I would go down to the orchestra pit and, with the curtain up, play the piano. One night Noël, crossing the empty stage on his way out, heard the music and stopped. 'Who's down there?' he enquired. 'It's Billy' I replied. 'I'm working on a new song.' He came down from the stage and said 'My dear, the middle eight bars are all wrong'. He then proceeded to show me how they could be improved.

The song Noël 'improved' for me was 'No Thrill', which was later published in England by Victoria Music, a subsidiary of Chappell's. This incident led to my playing the role of Vincent Howard, the orchestra-leader in *Bitter Sweet*. I owe a great deal to Noël. He was always out-spoken and seldom wrong. He gave me some candid advice about how to sing a song. 'Learn the meaning of every word, duckie. Then put your tinsey-whinsey little voice behind them and with your diction you will be heard everywhere.'

The Master had little sense of humour about himself. I was advised by his secretary, Mrs Lorna Lorraine, to be careful when viewing his paintings and be wary of my comments. If Noël said 'This is a little ship going up hill' that was amusing, but *not* if someone else had ventured the remark.

NO THRILL
Written and
Composed by
FELIX MENDELSSOHN
and BILLY MILTON
Featured and Broadcast by
HARRY ROY
AND HIS BAND
THE VICTORIA
MUSIC PUBLISHING COMPANY, LTD
52, Maddox Street, London, W.1.
Telephone MAYFAIR 3665-6
6

I once asked him to sign an amusing caricature of himself by Emmwood. He declined. Instead he sent me a photograph taken at a press reception in Ireland which was so wreathed in cigarette smoke I had the greatest difficulty in recognising who it was.

He arrived late at a cocktail party given by a lady friend. When she circulated introducing him to everyone, a young American journalist to whom I was talking, had his back to Noël and only half-turned when the hostess tapped him on the shoulder. She said proudly 'I want you to meet Noël Coward'. The young man replied 'Noël who?' This infuriated Noël, but two days later, the journalist was granted a special interview for *Time* magazine.

One evening after a performance at the Selwyn Theatre in New York, Noël took me to Muriel Draper's apartment; she was the author of *Music at Midnight*. I was about to move a silver lamé cloak which lay across a chaise-longue so I could sit down, when Noël hissed 'Don't touch that – it's been there for *years*!'

When I was young this Noël Coward lyric influenced me profoundly:

> 'I travel alone
> sometimes I'm East
> sometimes I'm West
> no chains will ever bind me
> no uncertain love will ever find me.'

So when I went to bed alone, I was sad; but when I got up in the morning I was glad; and when asked 'Why don't you get married, Billy?' I would reply 'Why buy a car when there are always taxis?'

Noël's personal magnetism made you forget the mandarin-like appearance: the big ears, the fluttering hands, the inevitable cigarette that led to a slim wrist on which dangled a thick gold bracelet. Those machine-gun utterances of inexhaustible wit could mow down the most vital of human beings unaccustomed to such verbal brilliance. His tongue defended him from any social or physical danger. It could console, destroy or encourage. Noel was a formidable friend and a compassionate enemy.

I feel that of the two greats in theatre – Noël Coward and Ivor Novello – one could be described as 'Dry Champagne' and the other as 'Baby Cham'. There was a gentle rivalry between them. When Ivor's new musical opened, the first night was very lengthy. Noël sent a cable to friends in New York. 'Ivor's show ran for three and a half hours – he enjoyed every minute of it.'

I have a happy memory of Ivor when he first invited me to dine at Red Roofs, his country home near Maidenhead. His other guests included Dorothy Dickson (leading lady in some of his shows), Bobby Andrews (his best friend), Zena Dare and Barry Sinclair (who used to play for Ivor whenever he went on holiday). It was an enchanting summer evening and we sat round the pool sipping pre-dinner drinks. After delicious food Ivor played my latest recording, 'Just imagine that he loves you dearly', a hit song from the American musical *Good News*. We had a good laugh when Ivor pointed out I had forgotten to change the lyric to suit a male singer. It should have been 'she', not 'he'; but the record sold well, especially with gay people.

I called on Ivor at the Palace Theatre a week later to thank him for a most enjoyable evening. After the show he took me on stage to listen to Vanessa Lee's recording of the new song he was putting into the show – 'When a Violin begins to Play'. The curtain was up and, as Vanessa's lovely voice soared out into the empty auditorium, I experienced a memorable moment of beauty.

But back to the Selwyn Theatre in New York. Once again Noël fell ill and was taken to Park East Hospital for another operation. I replaced him in the show. When I asked Danny O'Neil, our stage director, who was to tell the audience that Noël was not playing, he said 'You are!'

Nervously, I made the announcement and I heard the audience groan audibly. This made me all the more determined to make them like me. It wasn't easy. They had expected (and had paid) to see The Master. Happily I managed to please them. Noël's designer and great friend, Gladys Calthorp, was out front and after the performance came to my dressing room. She said simply 'Noël will be delighted, Billy'. To me, those few words meant far more than a thousand of the usual compliments. Noël didn't return to the show and I played for him throughout the rest of the New York run and also on tour.

Mother wrote from home that the Maharajah of Mysore had invited Father to India to become his Master of Horse and supervise the racing stud. It left Mother alone in London and she was missing both of us. To cheer her up I sent a selection of my press notices. The one she liked best was that of Forney Wylie of the *New York Press* who wrote (and I hope you won't think it bigheaded of me to quote it here in full) 'During Mr Coward's indisposition, his roles are being played by a young Englishman, Billy Milton, who has hitherto done only the number "Try to Love me a Little Bit" and a few sketches. Now we find him doing the musical hit of

The last photo that Noël ever gave me.

Marjory Moss and George Fontana as seen in Paris before coming to New York.

the year, "A Room with a View", in Mr Coward's place and if you ask me doing it infinitely better. Mr Milton possesses the youthful zest the number requires, a zest which Mr Coward, although also a young man himself, fails to list among his virtues. Furthermore, there are many who have suffered under the delusion that the "Dance, Dance, Little Lady" number could only be done by Mr Coward. Mr Milton draws equally as much applause and spares us some of the facial grimaces Mr Coward indulges in. Mr Milton's singing and dancing must be listed among the pronounced hits of the season.'

I wanted to throw a party to celebrate taking over from Noël, but wasn't sure the stars I had met would come to an ordinary party, so I announced it was my twenty-first birthday party – it wasn't really, but it worked! I was very fond of Marianne van Rensselaer, niece of Elsie de Wolf Mendl (of the prominent banking family), the well-known New York hostess. She loaned me her apartment for the occasion.

Among my guests were Cole Porter, Miriam Hopkins, Anita Loos, Clifton Webb, Marjorie Moss, George Fontana, Tallulah Bankhead (who 'darlinged' everyone) and members of the company. In addition to the many gifts I received, Bea Lillie gave me a handsome cigarette case with my initials engraved in gold. Noël sent me a birthday telegram. It was a memorable night, but I did feel guilty about receiving gifts under false pretences. Since that time I often use the ploy 'It's my birthday today' especially when I want someone to do something special for me.

One night high drama took place outside my dressing room door after an evening performance. I heard a scuffling and went to investigate. Miss Lillie, arms dramatically outstretched, stood in front of Marjorie Moss's dressing room door, crying out fiercely to a tall, dark man, 'Go away. You shan't harm my Marjorie.' The man was Ted Trevor, the American dancer who was trying to persuade Marjorie to become his partner. He had once forcibly entered her apartment, torn up every photograph except one of himself and beat her.

This scene culminated when Noël and Bea told him they would call the police unless he agreed to take the ship sailing to England that night. They would pay for his passage. He agreed and we all heaved a sigh of relief when he left. To celebrate his departure we held an impromptu party which went on until the early hours; then the phone rang. Ted was still in New York! Next day arrangements were made to ensure that he did not intimidate Marjorie again, and Moss and Fontana continued to be the ace international dance-team, until Marjorie married Hollywood producer

Edmund Goulding.

Ted Trevor eventually went to England and teamed-up with the always beautifully-dressed Dinah Harris and they started to work the smart cabaret circuits. They had a successful season at the Casino, Monte Carlo, but Ted gambled at the tables and lost every penny they possessed. Somehow they managed to get to London where they checked in at the expensive Carlton Hotel in the Haymarket. Ted telephoned and asked me over. He explained they were broke. I asked 'What happens when the hotel present their bill?' They had been there nearly a month. The audacity of his reply still makes me laugh. 'We'll offer to dance it off!' And that's exactly what they did.

The Carlton Hotel announced they had the honour to present the world famous dancers Ted Trevor and Dinah Harris, direct from their sensational success at Monte Carlo. They proved such a big attraction that their season was extended far beyond the point when their hotel account was settled. Sophie Tucker saw the act and signed them to appear on her variety bill at the London Palladium. Before long Ted was up to his old tricks again and Dinah left him. His next partner was a beautiful brunette, but when he tried them on her, she told her friend (a diplomat) and through this contact it was discreetly arranged that Ted was returned to America.

Prohibition was in full force while we were at the Selwyn. My dresser at the theatre was a good-hearted, ugly-gnome named John Butzie Carboni. He made his real money out of bootleg hootch – fiery liquid that could knock the eyeballs out of a dragon. It was said that his bathtub-gin could send you blind, ruin your kidneys and corrode your liver. But plenty of people drank Butzie's firewater and survived. On the profits he wintered in Florida. He didn't need the money he earned as a dresser, but it provided a good front and he really loved the theatre and theatre folk.

There were others who cut themselves in on his profits. A big Irish cop walked into my dressing-room one night and put his feet up on my table. This assured me his visit was friendly and not official. Butzie treated him with deference and asked me 'Got any dough? I want a hundred dollars.' I knew he only carried 'small change' around with him – if he were ever picked up by police, a large sum would have wanted explaining. So I rustled up the requested dollars which he gave to the cop quite openly. We then relaxed with some of 'Butzie's Specials' – best quality hootch in bottles labelled 'Gordons Gin'! Years later when I played the Rainbow Room in New York, prohibition was over and so were Butzie's big profits. I found him running a small news-stand right outside the Selwyn

A sketch of me done by J. Gilroy.

Beatrice Lillie in New York for *This Year of Grace*.
[RAYMOND MANDER & JOE MITCHENSON THEATRE COLLECTION]

Theatre. He had come down in the world, but he still loved actors and in his palmier days, he had so often helped them when they fell on hard times.

I visited Harlem one night after the show to see the Midnight Matinee for the Pullman Porters Association. An all-coloured show with the Nicholas Brothers, whose simultaneous tap-dancing routine climaxed in a breath-taking leap from the top step to the stage, landing in the splits. The veteran originator of the staircase dance, Bill Robinson, was also on the bill. He was the grand-daddy of them all and had taught most of the stars who later gained fame as dancers.

I was invited to an after-show party and the next morning, my head and I awoke in a coloured hotel. I had no recollection of how I got there or who had put me to bed. My wallet was still intact and I have always wanted to thank someone for that.

The Broadway run came to an end and our success was repeated on a tour which took us to Chicago, Detroit, Philadelphia, Columbus, Ohio and then on to Canada where we played London, Hamilton, Toronto and Montreal.

An extraordinary incident occurred during a matinee in London, Ontario, in a scene which finished with Bea Lillie singing 'Britannia Rules the Waves'. At the end of the second verse, the chorus were all ranged in an oblique line, well away from the centre of the stage. We suddenly realised that Bea was repeating the second verse, which kept the crowd glued to their places on stage. Luckily the orchestra realised what was happening. Suddenly a big arc-light fell from the flies, landing with a terrific crash in the middle of the empty stage, where, by rights, the artists would have been standing if Bea hadn't made the mistake. Without batting an eyelid, Bea went into the chorus and the crowd moved to their positions covering the entire stage. It was a miracle nobody was hurt.

It was at Montreal that Cochran cabled me to say that on my return he wanted me to play Vincent Howard in *Bitter Sweet* which was to open at His Majesty's Theatre in the Haymarket. This news made the crossing to Liverpool doubly pleasant. I was going home a success. I knew I had been right in leaving the champagne trade.

CHAPTER FOUR

Bitter Sweet

Rehearsals for *Bitter Sweet* were already in progress when I arrived, but I was bitterly disappointed when I was given the script. My part was small with only two appearances – the prologue and epilogue. It was such a let-down after New York. I was so angry I forgot that the role of Vincent Howard, who falls in love with Lady Shane's daughter, was the *essence* of the plot.

Next day I informed Frank Collins, Cochran's supervisor, that I had received an offer from another management, which was untrue; and as the salary Cochran offered, £15, was ridiculous, I would only consider the part if it were doubled. Collins said I was mad to ask for that sort of money for so small a part. 'In any case' he said, 'in my opinion *Bitter Sweet* won't run. The leading lady is middle-aged and the tenor is a foreigner who can hardly speak English.' Collins said that if I persisted in my demand, Cochran would never employ me again.

He was wrong. *Bitter Sweet* was an enormous success, acclaimed as one of the major musical plays of our time. Also Cochran agreed to pay the £30 I demanded and, in addition, allowed me to film and work in cabaret. As I was appearing only at the beginning and end of the show, there was a two-hour break during which I could do other work.

I shared a dressing-room with Alan Napier, who later lived in America and played a leading role in the highly successful American film and television show *Batman*. The other occupant was dark, swashbuckling Robert Newton, a fine actor and great elbow-bender. Bobby Newton must surely have been the original 'streaker'. One night after the show he went to the fashionable Café de Paris. On entering he took off his red-lined opera cloak, handed it to an attendant and before anyone could stop him, walked down the staircase in his birthday suit. Women gasped and waiters dashed forward to wrap a tablecloth around his middle. Unperturbed he surged forward to his table imperiously, like a Roman Emperor. The head-waiter, assisted by half-a-dozen underlings, carried him up the stairs and put him in a taxi.

One day after a matinée Bob took me to meet his friend Augustus John at his sumptuous studio in Mallard Street, Chelsea. We sank a bottle of whisky and realising that it was time to return to the theatre for the evening show, I called a taxi and suggested we have something to eat to sober up a bit. Bob declined the offer and dropped me off at the Hungaria Restaurant in Lower Regent Street, where I had lashings of fiery goulash which soon put me right, whereas Bob headed straight for the backstage bar.

It was on this fatal night our stage director Danny O'Neil put his head round our dressing-room door and said 'Bob, Mr Cochran says you've got the sack!' The shock sobered Bob so much he had to have another large Scotch to pull himself together before going downstairs to confront Cochran. 'You haven't heard my side of the story' pleaded Bob. 'Well, what is it?' enquired Cochran testily. 'You give me this small part. I have no opportunity to display my talent. It's driving me mad!' Cochran not only re-instated Bob, but later gave him a contract to understudy Noël Coward, whom he was soon to present in his New York production of *Private Lives*.

To celebrate Bob's new contract I organised a party at my house in Gloucester Road, Kensington, which I shared with Billy Noble, a school-master-cum-songwriter companion. I had written a hit number with him called 'My Description of You', published by Lawrence Wright. To look after us, we had a retired ex-army type called Rockle complete with quiff, army boots and halitosis. Apart from Bob Newton, I paired the guests as interestingly as possible: Dame Lilian Braithwaite with Pimpo, the red-nosed clown from Bertram Mills Circus and, for a contrast, Alec Halls the music hall comic with Basil Bartlett (he later married Mary, daughter of Lady Malcolm, who was a famous ball giver. The Albert Hall Balls given by Lady Malcolm enabled the servants of aristocratic house-

News of the World impressions of *Bitter Sweet*.

holds in London to have an annual Fancy Dress Dance. The affair soon became too fancy and too many people dressed and behaved like fairies. The police had to intervene. They *were* fairies.)

Bob was a wonderful friend. But if he didn't like you, strange things could happen. When he returned from New York, he co-starred in the American thriller *No Orchids for Miss Blandish* at the Prince of Wales Theatre with Mary Clare, whom he disliked intensely. One night, Bob, intoxicated, climbed into the flies above the stage and, while she was playing a quiet scene below, delicately urinated on her.

I came back early one evening from Elstree Studios, where I was filming *Young Woodley*, so that I could get a short rest in the dressing-room before the show, and caught Bob practising grimaces in the mirror. I said 'What are you doing?' 'Billy, one day I'm going to be a film star.' Every night before going on, Bob would try out his big melodious voice in the grand Shakespearian manner with these words, 'Oriana, life without you is just dust and ashes – I must have you!' He would then sweep majestically out of the dressing room.

Noël Coward, who admired Bob's work as an actor, put him into the film *This Happy Breed*, and had a clause written in the contract that read 'If Mr Newton is unable to appear when called, he will be fined £100 a day'.

When Robert Newton finally passed away, on a lovely pink-gin cloud, he was an international star. To prove it, he departed from this earth owing the Income Tax authorities upwards of £50,000. Whenever I dither about making a decision, I hear Bob's celestial tones boom out 'Do it first, Billy. Apologise later.'

I was waiting at the Ritz Hotel's Bar in Paris to celebrate New Year's Eve with some friends. When they did not arrive, I was very annoyed and as the midnight bells rang out I felt totally deserted. Determined to enjoy myself, I turned to the pair of conservatively dressed men standing beside me and said 'Happy New Year to you and success to all your plans'. They reciprocated my wishes and then suggested that I come with them to the Sacré Coeur to gaze down at Paris *en fête*. In the taxi, I became aware of a hand strolling up my leg. I thought nothing of it; we had all had a lot to drink.

When the excitement of the evening abated, they dropped me off at my hotel and promised to meet that day for lunch at Maxim's. I awoke with a king-sized hangover and, as I had to return to London that afternoon, made no attempt to keep the date. The holiday which C. B. Cochran had given the *Bitter Sweet* cast was over and I had to get back to work.

I had almost forgotten that evening in Paris, when a package arrived at the stage-door of His Majesty's Theatre. It contained a diamond and platinum friendship bracelet and was from Baron M. – the friendly man in the taxi. M. later came to London. He taught me to appreciate opera, ballet, good food and wine. I tactfully suggested that the bracelet would really look better on my mother and he agreed to replace it with a set of diamond buttons. He said that that was so I should 'blaze like a Christmas tree' while performing at the piano in cabaret.

Many years later I heard that he had been killed by the Germans while posted to Belgium. It was a great shock as I deeply valued his friendship and advice.

Boris Karloff and his charming wife Evelyn were neighbours of mine in Kensington. He was a very thorough man and a perfect gentleman. He told me that two actors were asked to do a test for the role of the Monster in the film *Frankenstein*, Bela Lugosi and himself. Lugosi, in haste to secure the part, made himself up, stuck two wolf's-teeth in his mouth and did the test the next day. Boris, however, consulted the master of make-up, Percy Westmore, and asked him how long it would take to create the Monster. When he was told it would take two weeks, Boris arranged that his test was delayed. When he finally did it, the make-up and character was perfection. This clear thinking and the combined creation of two minds made Boris Karloff a very wealthy man. Boris, whose real name was Theodore Pratt, gave me some useful advice including a little tip I found quite helpful on occasions. 'It doesn't matter how small a part is, even if it's only two words. Take it if the salary is the same.' I remembered it when I was doing some work for B.B.C. T.V. The booking department phoned me and apologised for the smallness of the part; a Vicar with only two words to say – 'Happy Christmas'. I replied, 'I'll say one word if the money is the same'. It was, so I accepted. It was the first episode of a new series called 'Till Death Us Do Part'.

When Warren Mitchell (Alf Garnett) saw me at rehearsal, he said to the director 'You can't have Billy Milton just saying "Happy Christmas". Get some choral singers and we'll make a gag out of it. I'll take a vase off the shelf, take out the flowers, drink the water, go to the front door to squirt it at the carol singers. When I see it's the Vicar, I'll swallow the water!' It turned out to be a marvellous bit of business. This episode was repeated several times and eventually sold all over the world, which meant REPEAT FEES! Boris's advice was invaluable to me.

A sketch of me as Vincent Howard in *Bitter Sweet*.

There was another occasion when I heard that a radio producer was casting a new show (which I presumed might be 'Dad's Army'). I invited him to lunch at the fashionable in-place for theatricals – The Ivy Restaurant. When we arrived at the cigar and liqueur stage he said 'There is a part, Billy; it's only two words but they are important'. The role was that of a Colonel. The two words were 'Absolutely ridiculous!' He enquired 'You have played a Colonel before?' I replied 'No, but I have played an Air Commodore'. I hoped that would suffice, but it didn't. 'Let me hear you *say* the words – with authority.' 'What here?' I asked in astonishment. 'Yes, here.' I thought he must be joking. But he was perfectly serious. So, in that crowded restaurant, I bellowed 'Absolutely ridiculous!' Heads turned, faces expressed amazement. In retrospect, I thought 'I've had radio series of my own so I'm bound to get the job' – but I didn't!

I played Vining, the dirty-minded schoolboy in the film adaptation of John Van Druten's play *Young Woodley*. The stars were Madeleine Carroll and Frank Lawton. The play had originally been banned by the Lord Chamberlain's Office; it was considered quite daring. Lovely Evelyn Laye, the musical comedy star, was a regular visitor to the film set and later married Frank Lawton.

An elderly character actor working on the film made me laugh when he said 'By the time I've got my elevators in, painted in my hair and got my truss on, I feel too tired to work'. He also gave me this advice: 'If you ever hear of a part you want, son, send this telegram to the producer – "I'm the only juvenile left in the business who can get his teeth into the part and not leave them there."' One day I did take his advice and sent a telegram to producers Robert Nesbitt and Joan Davis for a part I wanted in their show at the London Palladium. It made them laugh, but I didn't get the job!

Filming on *Young Woodley* meant an eighteen hour day. I was called at 6.00 a.m. and was on the set, made-up and ready to work, by 9.00 a.m. I finished at 6.00 p.m. and, two and a half hours later, it was curtain-up time at the theatre, where I finished at 8.45 p.m. My first cabaret spot was at 10.00 at the Carlton Hotel, after which it was back to the theatre to change for my last appearance from 10.45 to 11.00 p.m., followed by the second cabaret stint at 12.30 a.m. I was usually in bed by 2.00 in the morning.

To keep up this pace I gave up smoking and drinking. I was making headway: from a £4.10/- a week commercial traveller I had managed to arrive at over £150 a week – a lot of money in those days. To compare it

Pat Patterson (later Mrs Charles Boyer) and I in a sketch from a revue at
Grosvenor House.

with today, you would have to multiply by several times.

Following *Young Woodley*, I was loaned to Warner Brothers–First National for their film *The Call of the Sea* at Teddington Studios. Chili Bouchier was my leading lady and Basil (later Sir Basil) Bartlett and I wrote the film's theme song 'Paquita', which Gracie Fields recorded.

As work became more plentiful and lucrative, I had the pleasure of being able to buy a magnificent Packhard sports car, have my shoes hand-made and order a dozen suits from the top Savile Row tailors like Kilgour & French or Hawes & Curtis. But my greatest pleasure was to give Mother a new fur coat and Father a substantial cheque.

Then after more than six hundred performances of *Bitter Sweet*, plus records, films and cabaret, everything came to a sudden stop. As my bank balance was healthy and I was feeling fine, I decided to spend April in Paris to have fun and visit my old haunts.

CHAPTER FIVE

Paris with Mistinguett

I WAS FEELING YOUNG AND COCKY — AN ACTOR ON HOLIDAY IN the world's gayest city. Life was exciting, living was cheap and the future looked promising.

The name of Albert Tavel had been given to me as being one of the best theatrical agents in France. I thought I would call and say 'I'd like to work here', not thinking for one moment that anything would come of it. Tavel's office in Rue Marbouf was lined with photographs of famous stars and our interview was pleasant and short.

Later, at a café on the Champs-Elysées, I ran into Hughes Cuenod the opera star with whom I had worked in *Bitter Sweet*. He was very tall with an amiable owl-like countenance and a large adam's apple that went up and down like an agitated elevator, generally in the opposite direction to what you figured. Hughes was talented, with a voice of exceptional range, and was in constant demand for international opera. He too was on holiday and off the next day to stay with his parents at their home in Vevey, Switzerland. He suggested I join him but, although we were good friends, I felt I would prefer to be footloose and fancyfree in the *gay* city. However I proposed we meet that evening at the Ritz Hotel bar. When he arrived I found he had already bought the tickets to Vevey. So Vevey it was.

It was my first visit to Switzerland. The beauty of the snow-capped

mountains affected me deeply. I felt myself choking with emotion. I fell
in love with Vevey, with Madame Cuenod, with Ninette, her daughter – I
even fell in love with Grandpa, which was well within my capability.

Hughes arranged an invitation to meet M. Sandoz, the Swiss chemical
millionaire. He had houses in Rome, Paris, London, New York, Corsica,
to mention but a few. He also had a beautiful villa between Montreux
and Vevey. Sandoz had a collection of magnificent Fabergé jewels which
he kept at the bank and only brought out when he was entertaining
guests he wanted to impress. He told me he had an infallible method of
discovering his visitors' inclinations in sex. In the entrance hall were two
full-length portraits: one of a beautiful nude girl: the other of a handsome nude young man. Whichever you looked at first indicated your true
interest. On occasions like our visit, his male secretary (who was dressed
exactly like his master) was sent to the bank for the jewels and each item
was laid out meticulously on tables and displayed on different coloured
velvets. The measure of your personal success with the host was, among
other things, the measure of your verbal admiration. Next day the treasures
were returned to the bank to await further airing. It was a most extraordinary and unusual evening.

After a week a telegram came from Tavel, 'Private audition arranged at
Casino de Paris'. I was having such a good time that I wired back 'Am ill
will contact you when better'. Hughes reprimanded me, 'Don't be foolish,
Billy. You must go to Paris immediately, this is too good a chance to
miss.'

Reluctantly I left. When I arrived at the Casino I was astounded to see
that the 'private audition' was also being given to at least one hundred
artists. Dancers, acrobats and jugglers, all hoping for a part in the show.

Nervous and furious I went to the café opposite the stage-door and
drank two large brandies. Thus fortified, I told Tavel to inform the
management I must audition next as I had a plane to catch back to London.
This he did and the bluff worked.

I sang, danced and played the piano. From the darkness of the auditorium came a woman's voice, 'I want to see the Englishman'. And that
was how I met the legendary Mistinguett. The world marvelled at this
fantastic woman, one of the great international stars of her time. Her ever-
youthful legs were said to be insured for £100,000. King Edward VII,
who was an intimate friend of hers, had once said 'Mis, you represent
Paris for the whole world'. At the age of sixty-three she could still perform
an adagio dance which made the audience hold its breath in admiration

Mistinguett, showing off some of her jewellery.

and astonishment.

In my mind I had pictured her as a bejewelled exotic beauty. Here she was, dressed in ordinary blue silk pyjamas, a beret on her head, a small scarf twisted round her neck, and over all a beautiful mink coat. She made me feel like a prize stallion up for sale. Not one word was spoken while she eyed me up and down, turned me slowly round, felt my shoulder, arm and thigh muscles, then stood back to back to compare height. The first words she uttered were to ask my age; she then smiled and walked away. The audition was over.

Henri Varna, the silver-haired wizard of French revue, who was sitting in the stalls, called Tavel over and told him Mistinguett wanted me for her show. He invited us to his office to discuss terms. By the time we got round to the actual signing of the contract, the wine had flowed freely and the entente was so cordiale, I signed the director's portion of the contract, and Varna the artist's.

Despite the signed contract I still felt it was all a dream. It was difficult to realise that the mantle of her former leading men, Maurice Chevalier and Earl Leslie, was about to fall on my shoulders. Newspapers all over the world announced that *La Belle Mis* had found a new partner – Billy Milton. The French press said 'Grandma has discovered a new grandson'.

With unflagging energy this vivid, vibrant woman started to organise arrangements for her new super-revue, *Paris Qui Brille*. Before the show went into rehearsal, Mis decided to visit London to pick up ideas she could use. I hurriedly arranged her stay at the Piccadilly Hotel and a session with the famous theatrical photographer, Dorothy Wilding.

The first show we saw in London was at the Saville Theatre. Sitting in the right-hand box opposite us was one of her rivals of the French stage, Alice Delysia, who was very popular in England. Mis was wearing most of her fabulous diamond bracelets on her left arm. Spotting Alice opposite, she asked me to transfer her jewels to her right arm so that when she deigned to notice Alice and wave to her, she could give the audience (and Alice) a good look at her fantastic fortune in jewellery. Alice smiled 'sweetly' in recognition.

Afterwards we went on to the Café de Paris, the mecca of smart society. Mis was wearing a transparent black-lace crinoline gown which had been expressly designed to show off her famous legs. The place was packed and although the gown was suitable for her 'grand entrance' down the staircase of the Café de Paris, I thought it would be an encumbrance on the crowded dance floor, but no. She had it all worked out to her advantage; the crinoline prevented people getting too close to her, they stood their distance pausing to get a good look.

Mis took her ciné-camera (hidden under her mink coat) to the London Hippodrome when we went to see Jack Buchanan and Elsie Randolph in a musical comedy. We sat in the stalls and she had the audacity to film Jack's dance routines. He saw what was happening and, very annoyed, he complained to the manager, but she had already accomplished what she had set out to do.

I also became innocently involved in one of her pet tricks. I had no idea of her intentions when she took me in her car on a window-shopping trip around the smart hat-shops in the West End. When she saw something she liked, we stopped and she went in to try it on. To the delight of the proprietor she said 'This is the smartest hat I've seen in London. Billy, go to the car and bring one of my large photographs'. On my return with the picture, she wrote across it 'To the finest hat shop in London – Mistinguett'. Then, with the hat still on her head, she walked out of the shop without paying. This trick worked well in London, but I later discovered that in Paris they had got wise to it and it no longer worked there.

Returning to Paris we plunged straight into rehearsals. No one worked harder than Mistinguett. To keep her fit there was massage every day and this was followed by iron injections and exercises with a massive ex-wrestler-cum-apache-dancer who put her through a series of gruelling lifts.

During rehearsals I stayed at the small Hotel de Colissé, just off the Champs-Elysées. One evening I asked for my key at reception and smelt a most revolting odour of boiled cabbage. I complained to the manager whose apologies seemed never-ending. The reason he was so effusive was the odour, which had somehow percolated into the hall, was that of opium and I was too naive to recognise it. In Parisian society in those days it was smart to 'smoke' and in the room next to mine, the celebrated poet Jean Cocteau was being entertained by friends.

I had a friend staying in the hotel and one night we decided to sleep together. This led to a situation which was pure French farce. In the morning when the maid knocked on the door to deliver the *petit dejeuner*, I nipped smartly into the wardrobe in the nude, and as the lock on the door was faulty I held it closed with two fingers. Most bedroom floors in this ancient hotel sloped slightly and what with the weight of the door and the tilt of the floor, my fingers slipped. Just as the maid put the tray on the night table, the wardrobe door swung open. She gave but a cursory glance at my frontal nudity and calmly asked '*Encore un petit dejeuner?*'

One of the scenes in the show took place on the steps of Monmartre. Mis had a song which I accompanied on a barrel-organ. To prepare the organ for playing, the handle had to be turned thirty-two times. What I didn't know was that if I stopped turning the handle, it would play a few extra notes. It was something I couldn't control. At the first rehearsal, during a pause in her song Mis heard these notes and thought I had done it on purpose. Calling me all sorts of names, she flew across the stage, slapped my face and insisted we do it again. So I prepared the organ as before and off we went, but when it came to the same pause, it happened again. This time she slapped my face very hard, so I slapped her back. I was so mad I hardly knew what I was doing. Then I stormed out of the theatre and took a taxi back to my hotel.

When I calmed down I realised my inability to cope with her tantrums had cost me my job, plus the chance of a long run in Paris with one of the great names in theatre.

I decided to return to England that night and started to pack my things. But no sooner had I done so than the telephone rang; it was Frisette, Mis's secretary. She said 'Mis feels we have been rehearsing too hard. She would like you to join her for a long weekend in Deauville.' Relieved I replied 'Delighted'.

We travelled to Deauville in her car with a coterie of her friends, while Henri Varna's car took Oscar Dufrenne (Varna's co-director), Jean Sablon, Earl Leslie and Frisette. Later that evening Mis came down to supper wearing a pair of beautifully cut, midnight-blue velvet pyjamas and sporting the most beautiful jewellery I'd ever seen. We danced and drank and later I discovered she was still a force of nature and her physique was superb for a woman of her age. From that moment on rehearsals were less tense and apart from the normal upsets of any rehearsal period I felt more relaxed in our work together.

Mistinguett loved men; she drew her strength from them, and her vitality, both on and off the stage, was extraordinary. Her men had to be personable, young and virile, but the one real love of her life always remained Maurice Chevalier. She had discovered him when he was only fifteen years old, an unknown performer at the Folies Bergère. She guided and eventually starred him in her shows and made him famous. When his fame overshadowed hers he left her, but Mis retained her devotion to Chevalier until the last breath left her body at the age of eighty-two. Chevalier warned me against becoming too fascinated by Mis. He said

Programme for *Paris Qui Brille*, Mis's spectacular in which I partnered her.

'Beware of dangerous pity'. I discovered what he meant. You could become so involved with her that your time was never your own. She was very possessive. I steered a middle course by never being too subservient. Mis had little to do with women except those close to her: Frisette, her secretary and Jade, her understudy.

Shortly after our weekend in Deauville Mis gave me a present. It was one of the songs she had intended to sing in the show, *'Une Girl c'est Gentil'* which became my opening number. In this scene a line of girls were dressed in scanty Chinese costume with small venetian-blinds which covered their backsides. At the end of the dance routine they turned their backs to the audience (which they hadn't done previously) and, as they made their exit, pulled up the blinds to reveal their dainty bottoms. It was tough opposition for me.

One sketch which I played in the auditorium caused me a deal of apprehension. I had rehearsed every day with a white pigeon which was attached to a long length of string. The bird had to be trained to fly round the auditorium and then return to my hand. The creature was docile and easily trained, but evidently it was so relieved when it landed, it often left its 'visiting card' and, if I wasn't careful, on my shirt-front too.

One thing that did astonish me about the world-famous Casino de Paris of those days, was its condition backstage. As far as the revue was concerned, it was an unforgettable scene of flamboyance, feathers, tits, tinsel, satin and sex, but a potential death-trap behind the curtain in the event of fire. I'd hate to think what would have happened if there had been one. The fire-prevention apparatus was minimal and old-fashioned, perhaps they thought it was precaution enough. Excitement was generated one night when a young fireman was indecently touched-up by one of the chorus boys. The fireman complained to his chief who in turn complained to Mis. She knew quite well who the culprit was, but she liked him, so she said to the fire-chief 'Why don't you send someone who likes that sort of thing!'

The backstage staircases were wooden and worn and many of the star dressing-rooms looked shabby and lacked toilet facilities. I decided to have my room completely redecorated. I chose a chic paper in matt gold, and fitted new blue carpets and blue velvet curtains. A lady dresser was allocated to me, a dear old thing named Alice Rambeau. She would sit outside my room and do her knitting. One night I mislaid my jockstrap. It was late and I enquired 'Alice, where is my jockstrap?' Not understanding she shrugged her shoulders. When I demonstrated in mime she

Mis and I singing 'You're Driving Me Crazy' from *Paris Qui Brille*.

Mis and I doing her number on the piano, sketched by 'Tor'.

exploded with laughter and said '*Ah! Trousse-couilles*' and produced it from under a cushion. I had thought that working in a French revue would give me the opportunity to wear lots of exotic clothes. But alas, because I was English I was hardly ever out of evening dress.

French audiences are notorious for their lack of applause. They are alright when you get them going, the difficulty is to get them started. For this you had to rely on the *claque*, a band of men and women who came to the theatre nightly for a fee. You received the amount of applause you paid for. I paid little and got little. Mis paid a lot and received a lot. The leader of the *claque* collected the money when we were paid – once a month.

On opening night people came from all over Europe to pay tribute to the fabulous Mistinguett. The theatre was packed to overflowing with royalty, millionaires, bankers, industrialists, American film magnates and the smart set from London who had flown over for the great occasion. My big scene with Mis started by my playing a white piano which rose by hydraulic power from the orchestra pit. Then I sang a number I wrote especially for the show entitled '*Je suis heureux tout près de vous*', followed by a piano solo accompanied by the orchestra. Mis then entered wearing a shimmering white gown created for her by Molyneux and sat on the piano. When she smiled that toothy smile of hers, age didn't seem to matter. We started our duet singing 'You're Driving Me Crazy' and then went into a dance assisted by a chorus of handsome young men.

Everything was going fine until one of her diamond bracelets fell on the stage. Before I could do anything Mis started to grovel about in the footlights in a most ungainly manner, searching frantically for her bracelet. The music continued, the chorus kept moving and I continued dancing. Moments later Mis found the bracelet, got to her feet, smiled and showed it to the audience who applauded madly. She then rejoined me in the routine as though nothing untoward had happened! Mis said to me later, 'I couldn't lose that one, dear'. It was her favourite bracelet and had been a gift from one of her royal admirers, the King of the Belgians or the King of Spain, I forget which.

The entire ostrich world must have been denuded of feathers for her finale costume: a twelve-foot head-dress and a twenty-foot train. As she descended the vast staircase balancing the weighty head-dress and feathered apparel, it brought murmurs of delight and admiration from the audience. She deserved and got an ovation as the undisputed Queen of Revue. She also wore her entire collection of jewellery – diamond bracelets, brooches and rings – mementos of her vigorous and amorous life. She looked as if she could have settled the French National Debt and still have had enough left over for her old age. As a rival said, 'There's one thing to be said about Mis; she never had her face lifted, only her legs'.

Josephine Baker, the coffee-coloured singer and star of the previous Casino de Paris show, attended the first night with her entourage. She occupied the stage-box and looked voluptuous, obviously trying to distract attention from the older star on the stage. During the interval she signed autograph books and also photographs of herself (which her secretary had readily to hand), before going backstage to Mistinguett's dressing room. Josephine flattered Mis and enthused about the show so much that you would have thought they were life-long friends instead of bitter rivals.

Josephine and her friends then left the theatre, leaving their stage-box obviously empty, and made their exit through the stage-door where Josephine held court again with the crowd who were waiting to greet Mistinguett after the performance. Giving them a free, autographed picture of herself induced many to leave, so by the time Mis and I finally emerged from the stage-door, only a handful of faithful fans remained!

Beautiful girls wandering around in the nude except for a few beads, were commonplace backstage, and a voyeur looking down on the stage from the flies would have had a great time during a twenty-minute sketch played in an Alaskan Log Cabin. The villain had tied the heroine (Mis) securely to a chair, while a snow-storm raged outside. Then through the open window, leapt an Alsatian dog to her rescue. He was trained to untie knots and with much growling and shaking, the animal pawed and bit the ropes until he finally freed her. It was good, dramatic and very corny stuff. To avoid the possibility of the dog being distracted, all entrances to the stage were securely closed. This meant that the only people permitted backstage were the stage-hands and the semi-nude lovelies who followed immediately after the sketch. So, as they had nothing to do for twenty minutes, they amused each other.

There was also a Roman Chariot scene with Mis as the be-plumed charioteer. From the front it appeared to the audience that the horses were racing furiously towards them. The horses 'raced' on rubber rollers discreetly hidden by the crowd of supernumeraries on stage. Mis urged on the horses to greater effort by lashing them with a red velvet whip covered with diamanté. The sight of the dear old lady trying to keep two galloping white broad-beamed horses in check seemed to me ludicrous. Actually, she gave up playing this scene later on. I greatly admired the producer, Henri Varna. There was hardly a trick in the book he didn't pull to keep his ageing star in the firmament.

I've often wondered why Mis continued working so hard and so long, particularly as she was so wealthy. It appears her doctor told her that if she stopped working she would die. I think there was another reason: she loved money. In fact, she had a mania for money. I discovered she received a rake-off not only from the costumes, scenery, programmes, but also from the cloak-rooms and toilets as well.

On her birthday a revealing incident occurred at her house in Boujival just outside Paris. Every room in the house was littered with photographs of Maurice Chevalier and herself on holiday, on tour, at first nights, in the grounds, arm in arm, embracing: the lot. After dinner we all sat round the big dining table for the main event of the evening, birthday-present time. I gave her perfume, Dufrenne a diamond watch and Varna a beautiful white-fox fur. But the present that most delighted her was Earl Leslie's, a large wooden casket. On opening it she caught sight of a stack of newly-minted francs, which made her face fall like an old venetian blind. Then she saw that pinned inside the deep lid was a large quantity of high-denomination banknotes from every country that Earl and she had ever worked together. She was in seventh heaven.

Practically every night after the show we went to a night club, so that Mis could be seen. Her favourite haunt was the fashionable Bricktops. The singers Louis Cole and Mabel Mercer were the main cabaret attraction. Usually the place was so crowded the waiters had to slide their bottoms along the opposite table before they could serve you. Cole Porter made Bricktops his first port of call whenever he visited Paris and allowed Louis and Mabel to sing his new songs even before they were published.

Louis Cole had a passionate friend, the brilliant pianist Garland Wilson. Their great ambition was to give a concert together at the famous Salle Pleyel. When the concert was eventually announced, there was a big demand for tickets, a sell-out was in prospect. Sadly, when the day arrived, neither had the energy to get out of their bed, let alone give a two-hour concert. The concert was cancelled and ticket-money refunded. It naturally caused a good deal of gossip and some malicious friends suggested it was the very first time in the history of the Salle Pleyel that a performance was cancelled on account of love. But this was France – *Vive l'amour!*

Mis took me to a party given by the Rocky Twins. These sexy boys from Denmark had now become the toast of Parisian high society. We arrived in the middle of an altercation between the Bolivian tin million-aire Arturo Lopez and one of the twins. He had apparently refused to wear a costly pearl necklace which Arturo had bought him at Cartier's under his shirt. 'It tickles me' he complained, removed it from his neck and put it down on the table. In a flash Mis, sizing up the situation, picked up the necklace and said 'I don't like to see you both quarrelling like this. I will wear it until you make it up.' Whereupon she put it round her neck. No one saw that necklace again except in her private collection.

I nearly fell for one of her suggestions. Earl Leslie, Varna and I were at supper with her at Ciro's when she rebuked me for squandering money in having a good time. She suggested it would be wiser if she kept my salary in her bank and refunded it to me before I returned to England. Before I had a chance to reply, Earl gave me a kick under the table and an almost imperceptible shake of the head. Getting the message, I thanked Mis for her kind offer and said I would consider it.

Earl also told me of an interesting set-up at the Casino de Paris in those days. The girl friends and boy friends of the top management eventually became agents; a lucrative business because the commission on artists' salaries was paid direct by the Casino to the agent. It was a convenient way of pensioning off ex-lovers.

During the social rounds with Mis, I came into contact with the Dolly Sisters (Rosie and Jennie) through my friendship with Billy Reynolds, one of their ex-dancing partners. The Dollys had been great favourites in Paris and starred in many revues. They then opened a fashion salon on the Champs-Elysées. Whenever they showed their collection it meant big business. I never discovered the ingredients of the highly-potent cocktails they offered, but they sent the customers on such a 'trip' that the results were fantastic sales. The dancing Dollys made a fortune and promptly lost it gambling. Luckily for them there was always a Gordon Selfridge waiting in the wings to come to their financial rescue. They had a neat trick that usually paid off handsomely. Whenever they saw one of their pet rajahs or millionaire-friends approaching, they quickly removed whatever jewels they were wearing and gave them to Billy Reynolds to put into the tail pocket of his dress coat, and then complained bitterly that times were so hard they had been forced to sell their jewellery. Their boy-friends took compassion on them and generally obliged with a present of a new diamond bracelet or ring. Rosie Dolly eventually married Irving

Publicity poster showing Mis in the Roman chariot scene.

Netcher of Chicago, but for Jennie it was tragedy. She was found hanged, behind the bathroom door at her hotel.

Basil Dean the producer was on holiday in Paris, at the same time as star impressionist Florence Desmond. He brought her to see the show. He liked my work and asked Dessie if she knew me. Her reply was 'No'. Unbeknown to her, during the interval he slipped round to the stage-door and left a note asking me to meet him at noon the next day at the Ritz Hotel bar, to discuss the possibility of a film. I kept the appointment and was talking to Dean when Dessie arrived. At first she seemed to find it difficult to recognise me which was surprising, considering we had performed Noël Coward's 'Dance, Dance Little Lady' together on Broadway for months on end at the Selwyn Theatre.

I think her reluctance to acknowledge me came from an incident which occurred when she was understudying Bea Lillie and I was understudying Noël Coward. We were both watching Bea from the wings. Dessie said, 'Billy, wait until *I* play for Bea. I'll show you how to be funny'. She was standing behind me and without thinking I replied, 'Dessie, you are a wonderful impersonator but remember, Bea is a born clown'.

I have the feeling Dessie never forgave me for that remark. In fact I was told later by my agents, Reeves and Lamport (who were also Dessie's), that they were booking a variety tour and someone had refused to have me on her bill. I had already been successful in variety – Moss, Stoll and L.T.V. theatres – so there was no question of merit involved. As it prevented me earning my livelihood I resented it. The cause of the animosity I didn't discover until later. I am and always will be very fond of Bea. Apart from my thoughtless remark to Florence Desmond in New York, I felt there was also a small feud between these two stars. I told my story to Eric Johns, late editor of *The Stage*. He listened, then quietly and without my knowledge, went out of his way to elicit the facts. He later apologised for doubting the veracity of my story.

The meeting with Basil Dean was followed by a test, the first ever to be made at Ealing Studios for the Radio Picture Corporation. I obtained permission from the Casino de Paris management to absent myself for one day to fly to London. Earl Leslie deputised for me in the show, but somehow during the performance overbalanced, fell into the orchestra pit and was seriously injured. My test was successful and resulted in a contract for me to play in the film version of Jerome K. Jerome's *Three Men in a Boat*, directed by Graham Cutts.

Back again in Paris I rejoined the show and, without telling Mis, started filming for Paramount at the Joinville Studios near Paris. The film, *La Couturière de Luneville*, was directed by an American, Harry Lachman. My role was Mr Strong, a publicity man with a ghastly French-American accent. My co-stars were Madeleine Renaud and Pierre Blanchard of the Comédie Française. Filming by day and working seven days a week with Mis was exhausting. The reason I didn't tell her about the film was that I thought she might demand a cut of my salary for permission to film. But she did sense something was afoot because I was quieter than usual during our off-stage activities. One night she looked me straight in the eyes and said 'Billy, you are taking drugs'. I made no reply as I preferred her to think what she liked, rather than attempt to explain and complicate matters.

The French film technicians demonstrated their dislike of American directors in general and Harry Lachman in particular. Their ways were odd and devious. There was one sequence with a fountain playing in the foreground, which had to be re-shot several times because of a mysterious shortage of water in the middle of the scene. Then a diamond bracelet essential to the plot was 'not available' on the day it was required. It transpired that it had been sent to Paris for repair and wouldn't be ready for a few days!

Dorothy Wilding's photograph-proofs of Mis and me arrived from London. The long delay was apparently caused by the need for extensive retouching. I showed them to Mis who was delighted and asked if she could borrow them to show to friends. I heard nothing more for a couple of weeks and each time I enquired where they were, I was given an evasive answer. Finally I went to her dressing-room unexpectedly one night, determined to get the matter straightened out. To my amazement I saw hundreds of photographs piled up on the floor. Mis had had them all reproduced. I challenged her, saying that Dorothy Wilding could sue me for infringement of copyright. She laughed gaily and replied that it would bring me a lot of publicity! When I realised she didn't care a damn, I demanded a copy of each picture, after all I had paid for the photo-session and was never re-imbursed, and she had the audacity to charge me 6 fr. for each copy! We had a big row over this. I should have known better because Mis loved slanging matches and she usually won the day. Early on I had discovered that whenever we quarrelled, there were two ways of accepting the situation. One could say 'You are quite right, dear' to everything she said (which in itself can be annoying), or remain silent, which I found to be more effective. But despite her meanness and occasional abominable behaviour, I was very fond of her.

Mis opened a night-club in Cannes called *La Cage aux Poules* – an open-air place. She was worried because work on it was badly behind schedule and the workmen had to be rushed to get it open on time. The laying of the dance-floor was left until last and the wood didn't have enough time to settle properly. Matters weren't helped by the fact that it had rained heavily and the dance-floor started to sag in the middle as the opening-night capacity crowd danced. By the time the cabaret (Mis of course) was due, the floor looked like an old double-bed – up at the sides and down in the middle. Ignoring warnings of the danger and possibility of injury to herself, Mis insisted on performing. Come hell or high water, her public must be served. As her act included a lively adagio dance, it was a miracle she wasn't hurt.

Mis also owned a vineyard in the South of France – 'Clos Mistinguett' – which was located at Bormes les Mimosas and was managed by her good-looking son who was born 'above the sheets'. You can see him in the photograph standing behind the estate-bar while on the wall behind him is a picture of his mother.

Cannes has always been, during the summer season, an international meat market for hustlers, gigolos or whatever you care to call them. Virile or languid, active or passive, they are the speciality artists of sex who have catered for the needs of the rich and elderly since time began. At the Carlton Hotel there was a flamboyant ageing American millionairess who had managed to lure a handsome young gigolo to her suite. When they were in the nude the gigolo turned to her and asked 'How big is your bank balance?' She bristled for a moment, then looking down at him drawled maliciously 'Honey, it's a darned sight bigger than your cock'.

One of the Cannes regulars was Napper Dean Paul, brother of the much-publicised Brenda Dean Paul. A true bohemian, Napper had run out of cash and asked me for a loan. I politely declined. He wasn't surprised or offended and said he would send out his usual telegram to friends of his mother worded, 'Luggage impounded by hotel please loan fifty pounds Napper.'

The following weekend I was sun-bathing on the Carlton Hotel beach and Napper sat down by my side; he was drunk. 'May I sit with you?' he asked. 'Yes' I replied reluctantly, then closed my eyes and listened while he recounted how well his fund-raising scheme had paid off. 'Can I bury my money in the sand under your dressing gown while I bathe?' he queried. Thinking it was one of his fanciful stories and without bothering

Mistinguett's son behind the wine-bar on her vineyard, Clos Mistinguett.

to open my eyes, I agreed. I didn't suppose for one moment he really had received any cash. When he returned from his swim, he had forgotten where he had buried the money. I was awakened from my pleasant doze by his shouts of 'My money has gone!' Annoyed, I told him sharply to get a beach attendant to rake over the sand. This was done and to my astonishment the beach-boy unearthed over two hundred pounds in banknotes. I suggested, for safety's sake he put the money in the safe at the Carlton where I was staying. He refused to take my advice and later went off to enjoy himself. I knew what was going to happen and sure enough, at 4.00 a.m. my phone rang; it was the police. Napper had been attacked by three sailors and robbed. 'Would I go to the police station to collect him?' they asked. I thought it wise to give him time to sober up, so said I would be there at 9.00 a.m. At 8.00 the phone rang again; it was Napper himself, all bright and breezy. He had talked himself out of jail, had a drink or two, was quite unrepentant and ready for anything. Many years later at the Post Office in Charing Cross Road, I saw a bent figure wearing an old raincoat, leaning against the radiator for warmth. It was Napper Dean Paul.

I attended a fancy-dress-ball in Cannes given by an American lady who liked bright young people. During the evening two hopped-up young society Englishmen had a terrific argument which ended with one of them driving off at great speed to the villa of his friend Peter Spencer Churchill, where he razor-slashed every suit hanging in the wardrobe. He poured brilliantine all over them for good measure, then calmly returned to the party.

Meanwhile back in Paris a friend of Mis became involved in a drug scandal which shook Paris high society. She was an elderly impoverished Countess whose title was her only remaining contact with the grand life. For a living, she shopped for drugs and served a clientele of distinguished people. One day, very drunk, she collapsed in the gutter outside the Cafe Floré on the left bank. When the police picked her up and searched her bag for identity papers, they found a diary containing all the names of her clients and their requirements. Friends who were in the cafe and had witnessed the incident, immediately phoned round to sound the warning. That night many well-known people left Paris. Apartments were searched by the police. A sculptor cunningly hid his hypodermic-syringe in the clay of the figure of a Borzoi dog on which he was working. The police found nothing, but when they left he took a taxi to Antoine's, the famous hairdressing salon. Antoine was a friend to whom he could explain the

Jean Sablon, a great friend of mine, who took over my part in *Paris Qui Brille*.

Oscar Dufrenne, co-director of the Casino de Paris and Palace Theatre, who was brutally murdered in his office.

situation. As luck would have it Antoine was at that moment attending
to the hair of Madame Chiappe, wife of the chief of police, and she incidentally was very fond of Antoine. When he finished her hair, he begged
her to intercede on his friend's behalf. The outcome was that the sculptor
was fined and ordered to return to his family in Switzerland and take the
cure. However he couldn't kick the habit and arranged for a newspaper to
be sent to him weekly from Paris which he collected Poste Restante.
Concealed in the tightly-rolled newspaper was a quantity of heroin.

What shocked and saddened us all was the bizarre and tragic death of
Oscar Dufrenne, co-director of the Casino and Palace theatres. At one
time he had Mistinguett, Maurice Chevalier and Josephine Baker all under
contract. He was found dead in his office, murdered with a pair of scissors
by a person (or persons) unknown and his body hidden under a Turkish
rug. As Oscar's office adjoined the stalls promenade at the Palace where
Jean Sablon was starring in a revue, it was presumed that a member of the
promenoir had committed the crime during the performance. The
mystery was further complicated by the fact that nothing was stolen. I
had the impression that the brutal murderer was never caught but, many
years later while reading *Papillon* by Henri Charrière, I discovered that
the culprit was finally apprehended and sentenced to life-imprisonment on
Devil's Island.

Henry Sherek my London agent wrote several letters to me in Paris in
which he said that the American producer, John Murray Anderson, had
seen me at the Casino de Paris and wanted me to star in his London
Hippodrome revue, *Bow Bells*. A telegram eventually arrived which
read 'Can fix you Bow Bells and two pictures with Basil Dean'. This
caused me to arrange for my release from the Casino contract. My place
in the show was taken by my dear friend Jean Sablon, star of stage, screen
and records.

Before I left Paris I was persuaded to do a short cabaret season at the
Boeuf sur le Toit (Bull on the Roof), a name perpetuated by the composer
Milhaud in a sprightly composition. The French gaily described me as a
jeune fantaisiste, but my life was not a bed of roses. From my first night in
cabaret, bed seemed uppermost in the minds of those about me. Between
the attentions of the cadaverous manager, the elderly countess who looked
like a huge piece of puff-pastry and told me tedious tales of her youth (but
gave me countless gifts), and a wealthy business-man who wanted to give
me himself, the scene was strenuous. I managed to stave them off with
various excuses and avoided the business-man's repetitious invitations to

his *apartement particulier* (or peculiar if you will) to enjoy, as he put it, '*Un tout petit peu de champagne tous les deux*'. Finally when my season faded into the next sunrise, I was on my knees. No longer the *Jeune fantaisiste*, but a *Vieux monsieur*.

It was many years before I again saw Mistinguett. I was on holiday in Sweden and saw that she was playing in variety at the China Theatre in Stockholm, partnered by Lino Carenzio. Mis was still top of the bill and a big box-office draw. Her act started with the house orchestra playing a selection of songs she had made world famous: '*Mon Homme*'; '*J'en ai Marre*' and '*Valencia*', which brought her good entrance applause. The act went over very well. Carenzio was an excellent dancer, but he was very tough; he called her '*Vieille conne*' (old cunt) and other vile names. His quarrels with the ageing star were frequent and violent. Watching the show from the stalls I saw how he repaid her that night for a temperamental outburst. At curtain fall he brought forward a large bouquet which he presented to Mis. When she bowed acknowledgement to the applause, dozens of spoons tumbled out of the bouquet and clattered on to the stage. The audience was convulsed with laughter, but Mis could hardly contain her anger. I postponed my visit backstage as long as possible to allow the atmosphere to cool down, because I had arranged for a press photographer to take pictures of us together.

I sent the photos with a covering letter to Emile Littler in London. He replied by return that he had passed them over to Bernard Delfont who was interested. Shortly afterwards Delfont booked Mistinguett, Carenzio and myself to top a variety bill he was presenting at the London Casino – I was to be the compere.

Mis stayed at the Pastoria Hotel off Leicester Square, a venue popular with foreign theatricals. I called and knocked on the door of her suite and getting no reply, turned the handle, found it unlocked, walked in and sat down. She was completely in the nude, washing her hair in the hand-basin, unaware I was there. When she shut off the water and turned, she was astonished to see me. 'How did you get in?' she asked. 'You left the door ajar, you ought to be more careful' I replied.

As she towelled her hair, I saw that the intervening years had played havoc with her body – which was now like a wrinkled prune. Standing there on the carpet in her bare feet, her figure no longer had the impressive height afforded by her high-heels and hats. Though the plump curves of her thighs still had meaning, her breasts were no longer provocative. But because of my affection for her I felt compassion, not revulsion. After all that body had launched a thousand beds.

I had come to take her to see the American star Harry Richman, who was heading the bill at the London Casino for the season prior to hers. Mis wanted to get the 'feel' of the theatre before she actually played there.

Prior to the show starting, a couple, who for the purpose of this story I shall call 'Mr and Mrs Smith', were sitting in the row just behind us. Mrs Smith had recognised the famous star and tapped her on the shoulder. 'You are Mistinguett, aren't you?' Mis smiled and said 'Yes'. Mrs Smith invited us to have a drink with them during the interval. In the theatre bar Mis told them how unhappy she was with the silly currency regulations in England; she had barely sufficient money to last out until she opened the following Monday at the Casino. Mrs Smith, obviously anxious to get into her good books, suggested a loan of £50 to tide her over. They were coming to see her show on the Saturday and Mis could then repay the money. The offer was graciously accepted.

When they came round on the Saturday night and tried to get into her dressing-room it was so crowded with celebrities it was impossible for them to get near her. The identical thing happened to the Smiths the following week. This time Mis asked me to give them a note on which was written the address of her villa at Bandol in the South of France, where she was taking a holiday after her London engagement – the Smiths had told her previously they too were motoring down to the South of France – then they would ring Mis, fix a rendezvous and collect the money she owed them. The couple also said they would like to see Mis off at Victoria Station when she returned to France.

Mis and I arrived at Victoria with an enormous amount of luggage, including two hatboxes in which were concealed some puppy dogs she had bought. There was also her usual entourage. Mis greeted the Smiths warmly and invited them to join her for photographs being taken by the press. They were highly flattered and delighted. Suddenly Mis said 'Oh my God, I've forgotten to buy the tickets. Mr Smith, be a darling and get them for me. I will repay all I owe you when we meet at Bandol.' This he did though why will always be a mystery to me. The 'Smiths' were rich, well-travelled and worldly-wise, yet they fell for this three-card trick. But more was to follow. When eventually the Smiths arrived in France, they telephoned from the Carlton Hotel in Cannes, where they were staying. Mis said that by co-incidence she was motoring over to the Carlton that very morning with some friends, why didn't they all meet at the hotel? A close friend later told me of the finale to this extraordinary episode. Mis timed things so that her party arrived after the Smiths had started their lunch. As soon as Mis saw them she walked over, embraced them warmly and chatted while her entourage pulled chairs up to the table. They all had lunch paid for (of course) by the Smiths. That was the last they saw of Mistinguett.

The first house opening night performance was a complete and utter fiasco for Mis. In fairness to her it must be said that a misunderstanding about rehearsal was partly to blame. Someone should have reminded Mis that the afternoon had been reserved exclusively for her rehearsal. Normally band-call takes place in the morning and Mis, thinking she had to be there, got up at 8.30 to make sure she was in good time. The afternoon was not the time for her to have a lengthy and strenuous rehearsal, a woman of her years should have been resting. Her act had been scheduled for forty-five minutes of high-speed variety; this also threw her off balance, as on the continent the pace of the show was more leisurely. So the worst happened.

For the first time ever Mis forgot the words of '*Mon Homme*', a number she had sung thousands of times. Three times she started and broke down. I had to fill-in and tell gags to keep the audience happy while she retired to the wings to regain her composure. It was tragic to see this once great artist suffer in this way.

Unfortunately the press was there in full force at the first house and newspaper reports were brutal. The pity was they did not see the second house when her act went without a hitch. But it was too late. The critics had already put in their reports. One lady wrote '. . . I would not mention the would-be acrobatic dance the public watched in such painful suspense. It is heartbreaking, or it would be, if there was any necessity for her to be working. She is one of the richest women on the Paris stage; so it is not in order to make a living that she affronts the footlights. Is it the excitement or love of applause? The public would give her all she could desire, if she just sang in that husky kiddie-voice some of the old songs that she had made famous. Her act was far too long.' C. B. Cochran sent me a charming note the next day: 'Dear Billy, thank you for trying to save a gallant old lady last night'.

One of the numbers that did go well was 'I'm looking for a millionaire' which she sang as she wandered about the stalls wearing a fortune in diamonds. Each night as we left the theatre we were shadowed by the C.I.D. who waited until the jewellery was locked in the safe at the Pastoria Hotel. Mis had an enthusiastic woman fan, a rather butch-looking

Mis and I backstage at the China Theatre, Stockholm. She is wearing over
15,000,000 francs worth of diamonds and admits to being 62 in the
programme.

lady painter who followed her everywhere. Mis disliked her intensely and was annoyed when she found this woman waiting in the hotel lounge. In a basso-profundo voice she greeted her 'Mis darling, I 'ave painted your one leg in Paree and now I paint zee ozaire leg in London . . .' Before she could continue, Mis cut her short with 'And where are you going to paint *mon cul* [my arse]?'

Mis returned to Paris and carried on working with mixed success. Her final appearance was in 1950 at the A.B.C. Music Hall in Paris, where at the age of seventy five she astounded everyone by her vigorous performance. Seven years later she died. My memory of this extraordinary woman will never die. I consider I was fortunate to have had the opportunity to work with her.

CHAPTER SIX

Within the Sound of Bow Bells

THE JOHN MURRAY ANDERSON PRODUCTION OF *Bow Bells* AT
the London Hippodrome glittered with star names: Nelson Keys, Binnie
Hale, Andre Randall, The Wiere Brothers, Betty Frankiss, Freddie
Carpenter, Max Wall and Harriet Hoctor the Ziegfeld Follies dancing
star. It was a thrill to see my name in lights outside the theatre for the first
time in London.

Murray Anderson, one of Broadway's top-line revue producers, gave
me some good songs – 'All Roads lead to Bow Bells' and 'Love will
weather any kind of Weather' – but there was little opportunity to express
myself as I had in Paris.

At one rehearsal I was sitting at the back of the stalls swapping stories
with a colleague. Murray stopped the rehearsal and demanded I tell him
what we were laughing at – he obviously thought we were making fun of
his rehearsal. Actually I was telling my friend that the French had a
prettier-sounding name for the fundamental orifice than we had. The
French called it *parapluie japonais*. I could hardly repeat that in front of the
entire company, so I refused. This angered him and he insisted I go up to
the gallery and sit there until I did tell him what it was. I thought it
childish, but to avoid confrontation, did as I was asked. When I told him
later he laughed and christened me *Le parapluie japonais*.

John Murray Anderson was originally educated in Edinburgh, Scot-

Binnie Hale and I in a sketch from *Bow–Bells*.

land. He became a chartered accountant and then turned antique dealer before making a great reputation on both sides of the Atlantic for his extravagantly beautiful productions. Many of the scenes in *Bow Bells* were marvels of mechanical ingenuity. It was the first revue to have a moving treadmill on the stage, one for the sets and another for the players. Getting it to operate perfectly caused two postponements. Murray's assistant in the production was 'Binkie' Beaumont who later became top man with the H. M. Tennent management, one of the most powerful in the business.

When eventually the show did open, it was hailed by the press as being 'a riot of good things'. For my part, I felt it was a lop-sided revue with brilliant staging but the stars were left hanging in space. The show was overloaded with stars and for me, it was a let-down after my success in Paris. Frankly I couldn't wait for my 'three months guarantee' to finish.

I shared a dressing-room with Jacques Cartier, a brilliant dancer who scored a big success in *King of Jazz*, a film featuring Paul Whiteman and His Orchestra; which incidentally was directed by Murray Anderson. Jacques' act was a dramatic dance on a huge drum. He blacked-up from top to toe and wore just a loin-cloth and a tall head-dress of feathers. The three-dimensional lighting cast shadows on the back-cloth which made it both spectacular and exciting.

The real drum-beats were supplied by his assistant off-stage and there was an amusing sequel. One night the assistant had slipped up to the gallery to watch the show, and was having such a gay time with friends, he forgot that the next item was the Drum Dance. He dashed frantically downstairs to the pass-door to get through on to the stage, only to find it was locked. As luck would have it the supervisor, Charles Henry who later became top man at the London Palladium, was standing in the wings. Confident he could do the effects, he seized the drum-sticks and went into action. But Jacques' dance was more complicated than he realised; the drum-beats he gave fell before and sometimes behind Jacques' dramatic movements on stage. What made it worse was the audience who thought it was meant to be funny.

Other memories of the show are still clear in my mind. I was about to put on my make-up one night when Jacques grabbed my arm and shouted 'Stop! Don't use that.' He had caught sight of some shiny objects embedded in the end of the stick of greasepaint I was about to use. They turned out to be steel gramophone needles. I am sure I knew the culprit, a neurotic chorus-girl who had a crush on me. Incidentally, she also had a peculiar vice; she drank Eau de Cologne, which is ninety per cent alcohol.

[83]

Her mother, who was also a little odd, was a snob as well. She complained to me bitterly 'Mr Milton, isn't it awful, my daughter has fallen in love with a waiter – he's not even a head-waiter!'

The musical director of *Bow Bells* was elderly and found conducting twice daily quite a strain. One afternoon I entered through the centre tabs to sing 'All Roads lead to Bow Bells' and there was no music; the M.D. had nodded off in his chair. The first violin prodded him into action. He jumped up shocked. He then proceeded to take the orchestra through the number at a speed more suitable for a Mack Sennett comedy car-chase, than the finale of a first-class revue.

After three months I left the show to start filming *Three Men in a Boat* for R.K.O. Pictures. This was shot mainly on location at the Bell Hotel at Hurley and also at Henley-on-Thames. I had a narrow escape when my boat nearly capsized in the lock; the keeper had opened the sluices too quickly and a tremendous volume of water threw me out of the boat. He quickly leapt into action with a boat-hook and held the craft firm while I scrambled back to safety. The public watching from the bankside thought it great fun and part of the plot.

During this period, invitations to parties were plentiful. At one given by Elvira, daughter of Lord and Lady Mullens, at their house in Belgrave Square, Carroll Gibbons, 'Hutch' and myself were invited to entertain. Elvira had also asked The Three New Yorkers, an American close-harmony act who had scored a big success in a revue at the Duke of York's Theatre. One of them, Mr Barney, buttonholed me and enquired about Elvira. I explained that she was the daughter of Lord Mullens the banker and was crazy about theatrical folk.

Within weeks Mr Barney had wooed, won and wed Elvira Mullens. The marriage did not work out. It was said she spent their wedding night with her girl friend and he went to a Turkish Bath. It wasn't long before Mr Barney returned to the United States alone.

There was a strange and grotesque sequel to this affair. Not long after, I was sitting in a bar in Paris when a young Englishman next to me got into conversation. 'You're English, aren't you?' he enquired. 'You ought to have your hand read by the palmist sitting by the door. She's very good.' I thought it might be interesting so I went over.

The first thing she asked me was 'How well do you know the young man you were just talking to?' I replied 'He's a complete stranger to me'. 'Have nothing to do with him' she said 'he will only bring you trouble'. I was puzzled. Then who should walk in but Elvira Barney and she intro-

A scene from *Three Men in a Boat* – William Austin, Edmond Breon and me.

News of the World impressions of *Bow–Bells*.

Iris March and myself in a scene from *Three Men in a Boat*.

duced me to the man who had spoken to me, Michael Scott-Stephen. I'd
been told he was her lover. They invited me to come for drinks at her flat
when I got back to London.

On the appointed day I arrived to find the police were there. Evidently
there had been a violent quarrel during which (it was alleged) Elvira
Barney had shot Michael Scott-Stephen dead.

When her husband, Mr Barney, read the news in America, he immediately cabled the London Palladium and offered himself as a head-line
attraction. He also indicated by cable to Lord Mullens that he was prepared
to reveal the lurid details of his daughter's private life to a well-known
Sunday newspaper unless the banker was prepared to placate him
substantially.

Sir Patrick Hastings defended Elvira Barney at the Old Bailey trial so
brilliantly that she was acquitted. Instead of allowing the tragic and highly
sensational affair to fade quietly into obscurity, Elvira celebrated her good
fortune by throwing a large dinner-party that night for her bohemian
friends at the old, plush Berkeley Hotel in Mayfair. It was in very bad taste
and the popular press had another field day. Hounded by photographers
she fled to Paris. Some time later she was discovered by a chambermaid at
a small hotel where she was living off the Champs-Elysées, lying across her
bed. She was dead from an overdose of drugs.

I was asked to audition for Sir Oswald Stoll for a leading role in
Kalman's operetta *A Kiss in Spring*, to be produced by Norman Marshall
at the Alhambra Theatre, Leicester Square (now the Odeon Cinema).
When I finished, Sir Oswald turned to Norman and said 'Tell Billy
Milton he's engaged – I haven't got my teeth in'. Dame Alicia Markova
was the ballerina, lovely Sylvia Welling the leading lady and the principal
tenor-lead was a new Danish star, Eric Bertner.

On the opening night this much publicised romantic tenor failed to
impress with the show's hit song 'Red Lips unkissed are like a lovely Rose'.
He decided to get press attention another way. In the second act he deliberately slipped on the steps of the stage-staircase and finished up playing the
rest of the show hobbling around, leaning on a stick. The press next day
naturally gave headlines to the Danish star's injury, but they also reported
'With great fanfare, Eric Bertner, a Scandanavian youth, is presented as
the hero, but plain Billy Milton is the name of the actor in the piece who
steals all the thunder'.

When the curtain fell on the first night, Eric in his dressing-room said
to me 'In a few days time we will have another opening night'. I thought

News of the World impressions of *A Kiss in Spring*.

A cartoon of me playing Florimond in *A Kiss in Spring*.

this very odd. He was the big imported lead and his presence was essential to the success of the show. As it was twice-daily, his understudy Derek Williams played the matinée the next day and was excellent; he even received an encore for the big song. When I telephoned Eric to enquire how he was feeling, I casually mentioned how well Derek had done. Eric Bertner was back the next day! We all realised that with such an unfortunate start and a weak book, the show would only have a limited run.

As luck would have it, E. J. Tait of Williamson's Australian Theatres, had seen the show and was impressed by my performance. Wanting to show off a newly delivered suit from my Savile Row tailor, I took a stroll on a lovely summer's afternoon. As I was near the office of my agent Miriam Warner, I thought I would call in; she didn't even give it a glance. 'I've been trying to get you on the phone. Go at once to see Mr Tait at his Panton Street office – he can fix you something in Australia.'

Mr Tait offered me the lead in *Gay Divorce*; the role in which Fred Astaire had scored such a success in London. I thanked him but declined the offer. The journey by ship was over five weeks each way and, as I was doing well, I preferred to stay in London. Miriam phoned again the next morning to say that Tait had increased his offer. I gave her the same reply I had given Tait, I didn't want to go. 'Sleep on it Billy' she said 'I think you'd be wise to accept'.

I mentioned the whole thing to my housekeeper, a wise old lady who had spent a lifetime in theatre. She said 'Mr Billy, you can afford to make mistakes while you are young but you can't later on. And remember, you can always come home via Hollywood.' It was that last remark that sold it for me. So, to get to Hollywood I first went to Australia.

CHAPTER SEVEN

Australia - Bottom Side Up

THE CONFIDENCE OF YOUTH IS ONE OF ITS OUTSTANDING features. To think I was more concerned with the fact that Australia was so far away, rather than assessing whether I was capable of doing justice to the Fred Astaire part, now makes me laugh with sheer disbelief. I know that fools rush in where angels fear to tread, but the first-night notices in Melbourne proved it is sometimes better to be impetuous than look back with regret at a missed opportunity.

Before I left England I slipped in another film: *Aunt Sally* with Cicely Courtneidge. Tim Whelan (Frank Sinatra's first director) flew in from Hollywood to take over the picture. Presented by Gaumont British, the film was one of the most spectacular ever made in Britain. I played the son of a night-club owner and sang the hit-song 'You ought to see Sally on Sunday'. The score was written by American composer Harry Woods. His left hand was just a stump from the wrist, but he managed to play the bass part of the piano very well. 'Cis' was extremely funny as Sally and her performance was outstanding. This film was released in Australia to co-incide with my opening there.

I spent a few happy days in Paris before going to Toulon to join the S.S. *Oransay* bound for Australia. Aboard ship I met for the first time my leading lady Iris Kirkwhite, a pretty red-head who was famed for her toe-tap speciality. E. J. Tait had booked us individually, but straight away we realised that as dancing partners, we were not ideally suited. During rehearsals aboard ship she would often say 'Darling, don't grunt so much when you lift me or the audience will hear you'. But with a little adjustment we finally adapted our individual styles to blend satisfactorily.

There were interesting people on board during that long voyage, including the distinguished composer Percy Grainger and his charming wife Ella, and I often chatted with the international swimming-star Annette Kellerman, who was the forerunner of film star Esther Williams. Annette exercised each day, clattering around the deck in her leaden-soled shoes which she told me strengthened her stomach muscles in preparation for her Australian tour. The voyage was also enlivened by a gay old vicar who persistently invited me to his cabin to view his 'collection of coloured slides'. My room steward appeared to be permanently pickled but performed his duties perfectly. He told me he was married with five children. When I commented the long voyages didn't leave him much time to be with his wife, he replied 'You're right, sir. I've just enough time to kiss the wife, poke the fire and go back to sea'.

Gay Divorce was to open at the King's Theatre in Melbourne. At the bandcall prior to the final dress-rehearsal, disaster struck. Iris was running through her toe-tap speciality and decided to rehearse an encore. In some theatrical circles this is considered unlucky: a similar superstition to that of legitimate actors who will never rehearse the last line in a play, and music hall artists who dread anyone whistling in dressing-rooms.

Iris's tap-mat had been newly-painted, but it was not completely dry and as a result, she slipped. I was sitting in the stalls when I heard the ominous crack. A doctor was hastily called and he confirmed what I had feared, a broken ankle.

The management refused to postpone the opening night and insisted I perform with the understudy, an Australian girl called Mona Potts. We rehearsed feverishly through the night and the following day, right up to curtain time. Mona had obviously studied the part and knew the dances fairly well. I did my best to assure her and instil confidence. The set-back made us all more determined to score a success and that was the feeling when the curtain went up.

Next day the press reported 'By the time the final curtain fell, the unknown juvenile-lead, Billy Milton, somehow contrived to dance, sing and jest his way into Melbourne's heart. Mona Potts who, at a day's notice took over the part of Mimi, was nervous at the start, but by the interval was working without a trace of the nerves she had shown earlier.'

Leaving for Australia – we sat up all night making the horseshoe so that the press had a gimmick.

Iris Kirkwhite who was my partner in *Gay Divorce*.

Iris Kirkwhite and I in a dance from *Gay Divorce*.

Mona did wonderfully well in the circumstances. I thought her name
was hardly suitable for a glamorous stage artist, but she managed the
difficult routines very well. They were not the petty evolutions that used
to suffice in musical comedies, but intricate, elaborate steps and arm-
movements which needed long and careful rehearsal. I was particularly
pleased by a review that compared my performance very favourably with
Fred Astaire's, who earlier had tremendous success, partnered by Claire
Luce at the Palace Theatre in London.

Gus Bluett, the popular Australian comedian, played the part of the
Italian waiter, Tonetti. Gus was another of the long line of great comics
who enjoyed a drink. One performance he completely forgot to remove
the tray of tea things from the table over which we had to dance the
complicated 'Night and Day' routine. There were occasions when Gus
was unable to appear in the first act of a show, but somehow managed to
play the second act. When the curtain rose to discover him on stage, the
audience loved him so much that their applause was terrific, despite the
fact that his understudy had played the first act for him.

Drinkers are known to use strange places to conceal their bottles. Some
put them in the cistern of the water-closet, or pour their booze into a hot-
water-bottle and drink it through a straw. Gus tied his bottle of whisky to a
piece of string and let it dangle outside his dressing-room window. Gus
was supposed to be on the wagon and often, while he was on stage, his
room was searched by the stage-director who could find nothing. One
night E. J. Tait himself came to my room and hinted I was responsible for
Gus's condition that evening. I asked him whether it was likely that I
would encourage Gus to drink when Mona and I depended on him to
remove the tea things from the table before we danced the intricate
'Night and Day' sequence on it? He saw my point.

I knew who was making the trouble – the wife of the second comic who
was envious of Gus's popularity. She told her husband to buy Gus whisky
when everyone else was trying to keep him off it. With the untimely
death of Gus at the age of thirty-four, this fellow achieved his ambition
to take over the star comedy roles; but he hadn't the finesse or charm of
his predecessor and never attained his success.

Iris Kirkwhite eventually rejoined the show and we went on tour. There
was one seemingly-endless train journey to the mining town of Kalgoorie.
We played this small place because the miners paid such high prices for
the seats that it more than paid the company's rail fares and expenses to
Perth, our next date. When we arrived at Kalgoorie the place was buzzing

with excitement. The night before, in a bar, an Italian had hit an Australian, who had fallen and broken his neck. Furious, the Aussies in reprisal had set fire to as many Italian houses as they could. I saw the smouldering ruins of one wooden shack. All that remained was an old iron-bedstead and beneath it, a lonely-looking chamberpot.

After *Gay Divorce*, Williamson's engaged me to appear in *The Girl Friend* with the score by Rodgers and Hart. In the cast was the talented Leo Franklyn. Unfortunately there were many occasions when his behaviour on-stage was quite boorish so I decided to do something about it. There was some comedy business whilst he was on his knees, during which I had to seize his neck and waggle his head until the audience laughed. One night he annoyed me so much I gripped his throat with extra strength. He ran off stage and complained to the stage-manager. At the fall of the curtain I warned him that if he tried any more of his tricks I would choke him: that stopped his nonsense.

I had a terrifying experience during our season in Melbourne when friends took us on a picnic in the National Forest. If Alfred Hitchcock had been searching for a suspenseful scene for a thriller, nothing could have been more hair-raising than the situation which occurred when sudden torrential rain followed a perfect, sunny day. We were sitting happily in the car contemplating our return to the theatre in good time for the evening performance, when the rain struck with such force and volume we found the car quickly got bogged-down in the slush. We found logs to put under the car wheels to give them purchase, but we could only move an inch at a time. Thoughts about the possibility of missing the show grew with every passing minute. I had no understudy. One moment we had been listening to the uncanny imitations of the Lyre bird and watching the flying Parrots and the next was an inner panic which made the fraught situation into an insuperable task – a nightmare. We battled on furiously and managed to get the car on to firmer ground. Wet through and tired, the return journey was made at great speed and we arrived at the theatre with only minutes to spare.

My next role was Hughie in *Our Miss Gibbs*. When I read the script and heard the stylised music, I wasn't enthusiastic. But directly we went into rehearsal I found everything about *Miss Gibbs* had charm. Every performance found me impatient to sing 'Yip-I-Addy-I-Ay'. They tried to exclude the song from the original production in London, but it proved to be the hit of the show.

When my contract ended, I sailed in the S.S. *Mariposa* from Sydney to

Me in the 'Night and Day' number from *Gay Divorce*.

San Francisco via New Zealand, Suva Bay, Pago Pago, Honolulu and San Pedro. I held an au-revoir party aboard ship. Friends presented me with bottles and bottles of champagne and they armed themselves with toilet-rolls which were showered down on the quayside crowd below (an old Australian custom).

When we got to sea I noticed an attractive woman, dressed in black. She seemed to be alone. I soon got into conversation with her. She told me her husband had just died and to forget she was making a round trip. We had drinks together and she showed interest in my gold cigarette-case and lighter. I was surprised when the purser took me aside and warned me that she was known as 'The Merry Widow'. She did the trip regularly and by the time she arrived back to Australia would have acquired sufficient presents to make life comfortable until she was ready to repeat the exercise.

During the voyage, I rehearsed at the piano each day. Following our stop at Honolulu, I was playing the piano when an American voice from over my shoulder said 'I like that song'. It was William Davidson, a Warner Brothers film star. He had just joined the ship and said he was a golfing friend of Bing Crosby. He suggested we got together when I reached Hollywood. He said he would get Bing to listen to my compositions. This decided me not to visit San Francisco first, as had been my original intention, but to leave the ship at San Pedro and go immediately to Hollywood.

CHAPTER EIGHT

Hollywood Yet!

HOLLYWOOD IS A WORD THAT WILL ALWAYS BE MAGIC — A word that rhymes with tragic. I was reminded of this the day I arrived. I read in the newspapers of a beautiful young starlet who, for lack of work, had jumped to her death from the towering HOLLYWOOD sign that dominated the North Hollywood Freeway. She didn't know that only minutes later her telephone was to ring with an offer of a job, or so the story went.

William Davidson kept his promise and phoned to ask me to his home to meet Bing Crosby; they had been playing golf together that morning. I thought he wanted me to play piano at cocktail time (as many people do) so I deliberately delayed my arrival for half-an-hour and found to my horror that there were only two people there, William Davidson and Bing Crosby.

Bing was charming and unassuming. After listening to my songs, he arranged for me to record some of them at his expense. He also teamed me up with his protégée Marian Mansfield. Marian and I did a weekly spot on the 'Shell Hour' which was broadcast over the N.B.C. nationwide network from the R.K.O. Studios.

It was a lucky break to get in so quickly and I thought it would be wise to get a decent place to live and entertain. I rented a Spanish-style bungalow at a colourful estate called 'The Garden of Allah'. Nazimova the film star,

"NIGHT AND DAY"
J.C.WILLIAMSON LTD.
PRESENTS
"GAY" DIVORCE
WITH
BILLY MILTON
IRIS KIRKWHITE
MADGE AUBREY
MUSIC AND LYRICS BY
COLE PORTER
PRODUCED BY
CHARLES A. WENMAN
DANCES BY
EDWARD ROYCE JNR.
2/- NET
HARMS INCORPORATED
NEW YORK
CHAPPELL & CO., LTD,
50, NEW BOND STREET,
LONDON, W.I
& SYDNEY
CHAPPELL S.A.
PARIS
Separate Numbers
NIGHT AND DAY
I'VE GOT YOU ON MY MIND
YOU'RE IN LOVE
AFTER YOU
PIANOFORTE SELECTION

when at the height of her career, had built for herself this magnificent mansion, behind which was sited a group of bungalows which squared the garden and in the middle was a palm-encircled swimming pool. It was now a popular film colony.

My Australian friend Jimmy Watt, who shared the bungalow with me, received our first invitation to a Sunday lunch. It was a baking-hot summer's day and after several *Cuba libras* the twenty guests ignored the cold buffet as things began to develop and sex reared its handsome head. I lost sight of Jimmy. His parents had entrusted his well-being to me for his round-the-world trip. I was worried how he would take it all. Blinds had darkened the room considerably, and on the big sofa, it was like trying to find a body in a haystack. Suddenly Jimmy's face appeared from between a pair of shapely legs and all he said was 'This Hollywood hospitality is terrific!' Re-assured, I plunged into the deep end myself.

I made some very good connections that day, both heterosexual and homosexual, and was quite exhausted by the time a topless waitress – quite an event in those days even in the exclusive circles I moved in – came round offering us glasses of iced Vichy water. She explained that hitherto she had relied for her living on bit-parts in musicals, but that her boyfriend had persuaded her that there was a more handsome living, not to say more easy, to be had from acting as a waitress at 'funk-shuns'. She offered me her card and suggested that I should visit her sometime as she had 'just gotten in from New York a cute scalp massaging device' that would 'stand you on your head'. I thanked her and said I certainly would (though I never did). I watched her glide away through the throbbing throng of bodies, dispensing her cards with a balletic flourish of the arm.

I reclined in a plush velvet armchair, cuddling my glass of Vichy, to watch the continued athletics of the energetic crowd. It is not until one has watched, dispassionately, another couple making love that one can really understand what it is all about. The intense, repeated movements, the heavy breathing, the abandon, the sighs and the murmurings. How comical and how serious they were! It was there and then that I decided one could only enjoy lovemaking if one didn't take it too seriously. And I never have. My philosophy of the bedroom is always to go in accompanied by humour.

While I was sitting by the pool a couple of days later, a stranger got into conversation with me. He said he had just arrived from Mexico where he had been instructing both sides of the revolutionary war in the use of firearms, and he had to get out. He had been an officer in the British army and trained at Sandhurst. His name was David Niven. He went on to say that he didn't know many people in Hollywood. Wanting to be helpful and perhaps a little boastful, I said I would be happy to introduce him to some of my friends. He thanked me, then casually remarked he was playing tennis with Charles Chaplin the next day and was later having tea with Mr and Mrs Ronald Colman. You can imagine what a fool I felt.

With ten musicals and twelve films behind me, I thought it wouldn't be too difficult for me to break into Hollywood films. But I was wrong. Al Kingston, my agent who became a good friend, hired a publicity man and we got to work. First, it was suggested to the press that I had preceded Mistinguett to Hollywood as she was going to make a movie there. This was good for quite a few stories in the gossip columns.

Then I threw a 'Welcome to my Bungalow' party for the other residents of the Garden of Allah. They included Charles Laughton, Elsa Lanchester, Regis Toomey, Arthur Macrae, Evelyn Laye and Frank Lawton. Freddie Brisson, the son of Carl Brisson, the Swedish star who was a matinee-idol in England, came on later from another party. I had met Freddie who became a producer and married film star Rosalind Russell, one day when I was going to a B.B.C. rehearsal at the Aeolian Hall in the early morning, and bumped into him coming out of Asprey's. 'You're out early' I said. Freddie replied 'My girl friend June and I have a pact. Every time we have sex, I buy a charm for her bracelet. I must get one for her breakfast-tray before she gets up!'

Harry Lachman, tired of directing films in Paris, was now back in Hollywood and he and his beautiful Chinese wife gave a party for me. His home was magnificent. Outside stood his white Rolls Royce and he told me how he had acquired it: simply by writing the Rolls into every picture he directed, at a very handsome fee.

The same week Ida Lupino, whom I had previously met at her father's home in London, invited me to a party in Beverly Hills. Ida, the brilliant daughter of Stanley Lupino, is one of the outstanding members of that great family whose history in musical comedy, music hall and pantomime goes back to the 17th century.

The first guest Ida introduced me to was W. C. Fields whose reaction was to clasp his glass even closer to his chest, as though I was about to take it away from him. He mumbled gloomily 'My girl friend wants me to cut down on drinking, but won't say so. She keeps putting larger olives into my martinis.' He then turned and continued staring out of the window at the myriad of sparkling lights that constitute Hollywood's glittering

W. C. Fields and Sam Yardley at one of my parties at the Garden of Allah.

jungle, with his glass tilted at a dangerous angle.

Hermes Pan, creator of many of Fred Astaire's film routines, was the next guest I met. He was vital, volatile and full of wisecracks. He said 'Hollywood is a wonderful place when you're not working. You can go to the beach, lie on the sand and watch the stars – or lie on the stars and watch the sand!' He also said 'Success in Hollywood is relative – the nearer the relative, the bigger the success'. His wisecracks were oblique comments on the facts of life there. Next I was introduced to the much-feared columnist, Hedda Hopper. She was looking in bewilderment at a painting of two large squares. 'What's this?' she enquired of W. C. Fields who was passing en-route to the bar again. He gave it a glance and, as he moved away, muttered 'Balls by Picasso'.

When Louis B. Mayer the movie magnate arrived, it was the signal for departure. We were headed for Grauman's Chinese Theatre, the famous movie house on Hollywood Boulevard. Mayer was with his latest discovery, the embryo star of the film which was being given a glamorous premiere. The split-second timing of our arrival was upset, because on the way Mayer sneezed so violently his false teeth flew out of the car window.

A large crowd greeted us at the cinema, the forecourt of which is famous for the imprints made there by the feet and hands of many great stars. Rumour has it, that in the case of Errol Flynn, it was an imprint of another part of his anatomy. When we were seated and the lights lowered, it soon became obvious that Mayer's protégée would be 'permanently promising'. But to give her her due, she may not have had a lot upstairs, but oh! what a beautiful balcony!

In the insecure world of films, I found producers had two sides to their character. On the one hand they are as wistful as an iron-foundry; on the other, relentless in their never-ending search for young talent. One director, having some Hungarian blood in his veins, lured a Magyar beauty to Hollywood. Through my agent, Al Kingston, I was invited to the press conference held on her arrival. Among the many questions fired at her was one by a reporter who asked 'Have you had a checkup?' Pausing for a moment, she answered coyly 'I don't think so darlingst – just an occasional Hungarian'. Later that year columnist Hedda Hopper mentioned this lady's indisposition and said that some years before, she had been to a doctor who had diagnosed her illness as indigestion. Hedda commented in the *Hollywood Reporter* that 'Indigestion is now five years old and going to school next month'.

Film parties became so frequent I dreaded the morning after the night before. I would say to myself 'Phew, what an evening. If only I could get the blood out of my eyeballs and back into my veins again, I'd be happy.'

Hollywood was full of dishy girls who were hooked on the film-drug and couldn't break away. Even my temporary secretary had been a feature player, but when work dried up, had settled for secretarial work rather than leave Hollywood. Many girls worked as waitresses at the Brown Derby restaurant and similar places, because they were regularly scanned for potential talent. The talent-scouts knew exactly the types producers liked and when tests were finally run in the projection room, the successful girls were offered a six-months contract, with options. If they did the 'right thing', the contract was extended. The dumb but beautiful girls who were bad at dialogue usually appeared as hat-check or cigarette-girls.

My first test was at Warner Brothers. The actress with whom I was to work, didn't arrive at the appointed time; a message came through that she would be late. To keep me interested, I was taken to another set to watch a scene being shot of two climbers stranded on a snow-covered mountain. Three giant wind-machines were being fed with huge quantities of white confetti by the property men to give the effect of a blizzard. At a given cue, the male star was to shout 'There they are!' As he opened his mouth to do so, he inhaled so much confetti he couldn't speak. The scene came to a halt and was then re-shot, with one modification: he pointed, this time.

My partner in the test eventually arrived. She had obviously just got out of bed and had not studied a word of dialogue. This made me nervous and frankly I wasn't good. Later that evening, as I was sitting with Al Kingston at the bar of the El Ray Club, this girl came in. I pointed her out to Al and said 'That's the girl who messed up my test'. Al replied 'That's bad luck, Billy. She's the big boss's girl friend.'

While we were there drinking, William Kent, the American comedian came over to say 'Hello' to Al, immaculately dressed in a tuxedo. We both stood him a drink. When his turn came to return the compliment, he patted his jacket pocket and 'realised' he had left his wallet behind. He said he was going to an important party, could we loan him a few dollars? We obliged and later Al explained that Kent was having a hard time, so he did a nightly round of the clubs, drinking and borrowing a few dollars here and there as he went. The tuxedo was an essential part of the act, which lent credibility to his story.

I got a good publicity-break when Brunswick Records released a disc I had made with Marlene Dietrich, Bing Crosby, Gertrude Lawrence, Al

Jane Baxter, a Universal Pictures actress, and me in the background at the
Garden of Allah.

Jolson and the Boswell Sisters. Proceeds of the sale were donated to the Cinematograph Trade Benevolent Fund and I celebrated the event by throwing a party at the Coconut Grove. Among my guests was Lee Tracy, whom I met often when he swam in the pool at the Garden of Allah. He was great company, but wild at times. On one occasion in his hotel, he was fooling around with a pistol and decided to fire it into the ceiling. The bullet grazed the backside of a woman sleeping in the room above. It could have resulted in a fatal accident, but M.G.M. for whom he was working at the time, had the incident hushed up.

The parties I gave were well reported by most of the big columnists like Lloyd Pantages, Reine Davies, 'The Deb' who commented 'Billy Milton, the English actor has been entertaining with a series of swimming and supper parties at his home at the Garden of Allah. The other day his guests included Charles Boyer, Jackie Coogan, Ida Lupino, Ross and Sergeant Sam Hardy (who appeared in the film *Along came Sally* shown recently in Hollywood), William Davidson, Tom Brown and a score of others . . .' These reviews kept my name well in circulation and were considered useful and necessary.

This was also the year when the F.B.I. and press exposed a vicious gangster racket in the pornographic picture business. The method was to superimpose one picture upon another. Thus a shot of a well-known star stepping out of her private swimming pool, having bathed in the nude, was superimposed on another picture of an explicitly indecent nature. The victim would be shown the finished photograph and threatened with its publication in scandal magazines. It was a nasty piece of blackmail but it worked. These scandal magazines had eyes and ears everywhere. Head-waiters were heavily tipped for phoning through news as to who was dating who and reporting any unusual incident. Anything in fact that would stimulate the sale of their trashy, readable journals.

The head executive of a big film studio told me that one of his top box-office stars, a husky six-foot bachelor, was slipping because of many rumours that he was gay. The studio hastily arranged a marriage to the secretary of the star's agent, who incidentally was also gay. She provided a perfect partner in what the French so delicately describe as a *mariage blanc*.

The wedding brought world-wide publicity. The papers showed pictures of the bride, looking beautiful all in white, and the groom who appeared white, and all in!

Things went well for two years, then disaster struck when the wife announced she had really fallen in love with her husband, and demanded sex. His inability to comply turned her love to hate. During bitter quarrels, she threatened divorce and the revelation of the true cause of incompatibility to the press. This was thwarted by the agent inducing her to agree to the acceptance of a substantial yearly settlement. This continued for ten years, during which time she spent lavishly and reverted to her normal way of life with her girl friends. She also developed a liking for alcohol.

The situation eventually went from very bad to much worse. A well-known publisher offered her an enormous advance royalty for a book telling *all*. She phoned her husband to put him in the picture. After listening to her threats, he said politely 'Publish and be fucked! I don't care any more.'

One of the most unusual evenings I spent in Hollywood started at the Fifty-Fifty-Club where I went with cabaret singer Phyllis Clare. It was nearly 4.00 in the morning when Phyllis nudged me as I was nodding off, and said a friend of hers had just arrived and wanted us to go to his home at Cold Water Canyon, for a night cap. He was a big star in films, Phillips Holmes. The picture that made him world famous was the version of Theodore Dreiser's *An American Tragedy*. When I got my tired eyes into focus, I could hardly believe what I saw. There he sat, wearing a blue overcoat over blue silk pyjamas, blue leather bedroom slippers and a bowler hat!

At his house, the three of us put ourselves outside a large bottle of brandy, while Phyllis related the sad story of her being deserted by her current boy-friend Jack Donahue; then we all slept in Phillips' bed.

The next morning at the crack of noon, we were rudely awakened by an elderly lady who kept repeating loudly 'Phillips, what's going on here? I want an explanation!' It was his mother, Mrs Taylor Holmes, the well-known Broadway actress. Phyllis got the giggles and wrapping me and herself in the eiderdown, we tottered to the bathroom and bathed; keeping out of the way while mother and son had a row.

At 2.00 in the afternoon we had breakfast, with mother and son sitting at opposite ends of the table, glaring at each other, not saying a word. 'Silly old bitch' said Phyllis to me in a stage-whisper. 'I know her well, we've played together on Broadway.' There was still no comment from Mrs Holmes other than 'Pack your bags Phillips, you are to leave this house at once. I'm telling your father about this!' It was all too embarrassing for words. Knowing what pros are, I thought I'd ease the tension by asking Mrs Holmes for her autograph and her son for a photograph. This

Phillips Holmes, a friend, who later acted with me in *The Dominant Sex* at Elstree Studios.

helped to thaw the atmosphere. Fate was to arrange that a few years later, Phillips and I were to co-star with Diana Churchill in a film to be made at Elstree called *The Dominant Sex*.

Bing Crosby's lyric writer, Roy Turk, wrote a song with me called 'Half Hearted Love' for my spot on the 'Shell Hour' radio show. We wanted Arthur Johnson, Roy's usual composer-partner, to hear it, so we decided to drive over to Arthur's house in Beverly Hills one afternoon. As we walked through the rooms, our rubber-soled shoes making no noise, we came upon a blissful scene being played out on a comfortable sofa. There was Arthur reclining gracefully full length, eyes closed, with a seraphic grin on his face, whilst the daughter of one of the most powerful men in Hollywood studios, was gently fellating him. As she had her back to us, we retired unnoticed. Now, every time I hear the song 'Cocktails for Two' I recall this summer idyll and smile.

Al Kingston arranged a test for me at Universal Studios for *The Great Ziegfeld*. The way it was conducted greatly impressed me. First I was seated at a grand piano. Then the director walked slowly round me, firing very personal questions while the cameras rolled. In that way he got every reaction. I followed with a song and dance. At last the test proved successful. Terms were discussed and agreed. I was to sing one of the big songs in the film – 'A Pretty Girl is like a Melody'. Anthony Maguire was to direct.

Al and I celebrated – this was a real break. But we celebrated too soon. Fate stepped in. Before I signed the contract, Universal sold the rights of *The Great Ziegfeld* to M.G.M. and the picture was postponed for a year. It was a shattering blow for me and even worse for Harriet Hoctor, the ballet dancer from *Bow Bells*, who had already waited a year in Hollywood for the picture to start. This made me realise that my wait for a break in films had been too long and too expensive. I was still working on the 'Shell Oil Hour' broadcast series, but when that came to an end I decided to take the Santa Fé Special to New York.

CHAPTER NINE

New York

In new york i stayed at the barbizon plaza hotel. i performed in their revue *Sunday Nights at Nine* because they gave you a room
and a continental breakfast free. The Sunday revue cast included Shirley
Booth and those Danish dandies, the Rocky Twins.

Richard Krakeur became my personal manager and he got me on to
the important Corbina Wright radio show 'Our Hostess Hour'. To this
day I'm not too sure about a notice in the top show-biz paper *Variety*
which described me as 'Speciality in the Dwight Fiske manner, a stylist of
the popular warbling school whose pipes sound good when he sticks to the
song itself'.

Leonard Silman, who discovered Henry Fonda, Van Johnson and Eartha
Kitt, happened to catch my act at the Barbizon Plaza and signed me for
his New Faces Revue, *Fools Rush In*, at the Playhouse Theatre, East 48th
Street. He also engaged comedienne Imogene Coca; Richard Whorf,
later star and director for Warner Brothers; glamorous Betzi Beaton; and
Charles Walters, who was to direct Judy Garland in years to come. I was
the only Englishman in the cast.

There was a great deal of talent in the show, but it was not the success
it deserved to be owing to insufficient backing by Marilyn Miller and
Jimmy (Woolworth) Donahue. The show was not given a chance to run-
in properly. We also opened too early. For reasons known only to himself,

William Brady, owner and manager of the Playhouse, decided to open a week early and he put on a special Sunday night show for the press. The notices were generally good. Robert Coleman reported 'First nighters found it to their liking and were not backward in expressing their pleasure'. Walter Winchell wrote 'Billy Milton deserves first mention'.

Audiences enjoyed the show, but it needed money to keep it going until the word got round and brought in the crowds. In the meantime we limped along. A Texan millionaire, hearing of our cash problem, said he might keep the show going if he could see a matinée performance. We already had to cancel a matinée because the musicians union demanded a guarantee of payment, which the management couldn't meet. The electricians had also walked out for the same reason, so we were left with only one working-light and no orchestra.

Will Irwin, the composer, volunteered to accompany the show and so we put it on for an audience of one. The Texan, wearing a large stetson hat and chewing gum continuously, sat alone in the stalls for the entire two and a half hours. When we finished, he stood up, stretched himself and said 'You've got a mighty fine show here'. He then walked out of the theatre and we never saw him again!

As luck would have it, the Narvarro Hotel on Central Park South wanted a piano act and emcee for their new cabaret room, the Normandie, described as a 'Chic restaurant for the elite of New York'. I got the job. The opening night attracted a crowd of socialites including glamorous Marilyn Miller and pretty Marianne van Rensselaer, with whom I proceeded to fall in love. An added attraction was Haywood Powers, who could boast a line-o-type in the social register. Haywood Powers and His Society Orchestra featuring debutante Gay Adams, was soon established as an addition to the ranks of those of the upper-crust who thought it was the 'in-thing' to be of the world of entertainment.

My stint was three shows a night – 10.00 p.m., 12.00 p.m. and 2.00 a.m. This meant that with the Barbizon Plaza, I did four shows on a Sunday. I worked at a white mini-piano, and to its back I attached a large square of wood, and invited celebrities to inscribe their autograph. I also persuaded them to sign a miniature baby-grand piano, which I later auctioned for charity.

An eccentric and wealthy colonel was a regular patron. The hotel manager said he would appreciate it if, every time I passed the Colonel's table, I would halt, stand to attention and salute him. He would then give me $10.00. The Colonel loved this nonsense and after all his $10.00 several

The table advertisement of my act at El Morocco.

Billy Milton, Marilyn Miller and Joseph M. Schenk at a party at El Morocco.

times a night, was a useful extra for me.

Oliver Wakefield, the English comedian whose gimmick was never to finish a gag, was the attraction at El Morocco Club on East 59th Street, a watering hole for the rich. Oliver was a good friend, so I often nipped over in a taxi to catch his act before my last show at 2.00 a.m.

One night at the Normandie, I unwittingly annoyed a man who, I later discovered, was Leonard MacBain, manager of El Morocco, who was in seeing my show. I had already done three performances that night, plus singing requests at patrons' tables during the interval, when the band took a rest. It was nearly 4.00 in the morning when MacBain asked for more. I said 'I'm sorry, even if you were the King of Siam, I couldn't sing another note'. He complained to the manager, who fortunately took my part.

The next night at El Morocco I was sitting with Oliver Wakefield sipping Scotch, when I heard someone announce 'We have with us tonight the Master of Ceremonies of the Normandie Club. I'm sure he will honour us with a song – Billy Milton!'

The shock of this sudden announcement brought me to my feet to acknowledge the applause. I went over to the piano and did my act. Whether MacBain did this to get his own back for the previous night's wrangle, I shall never know; but he did me a good turn. My act went so well the owner, John Perona, offered me a season at El Morocco.

El Morocco was a favourite place of the late-hour smart set. The atmosphere was perfect, the decor elegant, with zebra-striped banquettes, stars twinkling in a ceiling of blue, and miniature palm trees. Irving Rose and His Orchestra, alternating with Nano Rodrigo's Rumba Orchestra, played tirelessly through the night. Luckily I hit it off with the New York night-lifers. Leo Marsh's *Night Club* reported 'John Perona's El Morocco is functioning in a lively manner these nights. Billy Milton, singing lyrical songs, has added new zest to this swank spot. One of the livelier parties took place last week with Libby Holman, Marilyn Miller, Chet O'Brien, Marlene Dietrich and Jack Buchanan (just off the boat from Europe) participating.' Louis Sobel's 'Voice of Broadway' column gossiped 'Marianne van Rensselaer nestles close to her fiancé, Billy Milton'. Ed Sullivan's influential 'Broadway' column noted 'Billy Milton at El Morocco has more personality than any of the British performers here'.

Marlene Dietrich was a regular visitor. One night I asked her, as a special favour to me, to sing 'Falling in Love Again'. She agreed on one condition – that she could hear a pin drop before she started. Her performance added lustre to my evening.

[117]

Marilyn Miller was another regular. While in her early twenties she joined Ziegfeld and he groomed the young, enchanting talent into a mighty star; the most dazzling show personality on Broadway. While co-starring with Clifton Webb in the Hassard Short revue *As Thousands Cheer*, Marilyn met and fell in love with Chet O'Brien, a chorus boy delegated to hold the curtain for her when she went through to take a call. He was tall, dark and handsome and Marilyn walked out of the show to marry him. As a wedding gift she gave him a big Cadillac car, a large wardrobe of good clothes and a handsome expense account.

The marriage didn't work out, and Marilyn became worried by rumours that her new husband was cheating on her. They quarrelled with ever-increasing frequency. She came to El Morocco practically every night and I did my best to console her. When my last show was over, I made it my business to dance with her until the effects of the many cocktails she had before dinner had worn off. Marilyn begged me to quit my hotel and stay with them at their apartment at Central Park, which I did. I was a buffer between two warring parties, but as I liked them both, it didn't bother me: except when their arguments went on long into the night, penetrating the wall of my guest-room and depriving me of sleep. My efforts were useless and the final breaking point came when Chet, without thinking, offered Marilyn a cigarette from a gold case identical to the one she had given him. But this case was inscribed 'With Love from Cliff' (Webb). Despite her wealth and success, Marilyn died when only thirty four.

Behind each banquette at El Morocco lay a steam radiator. When they got too hot they emitted a hissing noise. Every Monday was 'Rudy Vallee Night' and the famous crooner brought along some of his star friends to entertain. I got the impression that he was very conceited (I may be wrong). Anyway, it happened that one night while he was singing, the radiator behind where I was sitting, started to hiss. Rudy heard it, couldn't quite make out where the noise was coming from and suspected it was me. Unfortunately, during another pause in his song, it happened again and this time he knew definitely it came from the direction of my table. He was livid. I'm sure if John Perona hadn't intervened and convinced him it was the radiator and not me, we would have come to blows.

Cabaret star Dwight Fiske was famed for his sophisticated songs and it came as a surprise to me when a newspaper critic described my impression of him as 'A vicious parody of Fiske'. I met him at a party given in my honour by Marion de Wolf – he'd also read the report – and we arranged to play it up into a so-called feud. As a result of this, he filled the Savoy

My new passport photograph.

Plaza Hotel and I filled El Morocco, with people anxious to hear what we might say about each other. We both had a good laugh and he sent me a photograph inscribed 'To Billy – who knows so much – it frightens me!'

The songs the audience most requested were 'Hollywood Stinks', 'Yesterday an Egg. Tomorrow a Feather Duster' and the tale of the two elephants 'Jessie and Bessie'.

I know you can't eat press-cuttings, but they do a lot for the ego and the New York critics had been kind to me. So I made up a selection and sent them off to English film companies and theatre managements to promote interest.

Although I was having a marvellous time, there were occasions when I got homesick and longed to mix with ordinary people again. It was a rich diet – the super-smart-set each night, such as Joseph M. Schenck, Peggy Hopkins Joyce, Clifton Webb, Contessa di Frasso, etcetera, etcetera. To get away from it all, I would sometimes put a coat over the white tie and tails, turn up the collar and walk through the deserted streets at 4.00 a.m., right down to Wall Street and gaze across the water at the Statue of Liberty looming in the distance. En route I passed the Valerie Mission Hall where the down-and-out bums and meth-drinkers could get a handout of sausages and mash, and find shelter for the night. It was a sharp contrast to the vapid gyrations of the set I had to entertain nightly to get my bread. Having seen life-in-the-raw and the unbalance of it all, I went back to my hotel.

I realised it was about time I did something about renewing my entry permit. What a fool I was, I didn't know what I was letting myself in for. I wrote to San Pedro where I had landed, and for my trouble received a curt notice to present myself immediately at Ellis Island.

There immigrants and aliens were investigated and sometimes held. A bunch of sinister-looking gentlemen fired questions at me from all angles. No wonder they were suspicious of me. Until that moment I hadn't realised my passport had not been altered. I was still travelling as a wine merchant! I finally convinced them it was a genuine oversight. They allowed me to finish the season at El Morocco, but directly after, I was to take the next ship home.

So instead of being able to follow-up my success in New York, I found myself on the S.S. *America*, sailing back to England. It was as fate intended. Unbeknown to me, I was coming home to a handsome film contract.

CHAPTER TEN

London-Filming

FUNDS WERE LOW – I HAD TO PAY HEAVY INCOME-TAX BEFORE leaving America. I know money isn't everything but it does quieten the nerves, and the only way to get more is to give more. In London I stayed at the Savoy Hotel and gave a party, inviting the press, agents and film-starlets.

It was amusing to see the agents circling round the girls with the same tireless insistence as vultures hovering over a kill. There was an aggressive busty press-lady (the kind that seem a little closer to you than they really are) who said 'For one so young you look remarkably old in this photograph'. To which I politely replied 'I'm ten years younger than you are, dear, how old are you?' Later experience taught me how to handle the bitchy remarks. The press are mostly friendly, but there are some that you have to take with a pinch of pheno-barbitone.

The notices I'd sent from the New York Press had rung bells. British International Pictures was interested and Connie, my agent, arranged for me to meet their director of production, Walter C. Mycroft, at the Elstree Studio. The interview was conducted in style, compliments flew and a three year option contract was drawn up and signed.

I moved from the Savoy Hotel and rented a flat at Hertford Court in Shepherd Market, Mayfair, which belonged to Freddie Carpenter the dancer, later director. The decor was exotic: black walls and carpets, and

My favourite picture of June Clyde, who co-starred with me in *King of the Castle*.

magenta curtains. My neighbours were Rex Harrison on one side and Richard Llewellyn (author of *How Green Was My Valley*) on the other. Richard was assistant director on one of my films and I used to drive him to the studios each day.

Music Hath Charms was the first film I made under the new contract. It featured Henry Hall and the B.B.C. Dance Orchestra. Henry was a charming man but rather absent-minded. We were talking on the set one day and when the conversation finished he turned to walk away, forgot he was standing on a high rostrum and promptly fell off.

My secretary, Molly Hart, persuaded me (against my better judgement) to let her start a Billy Milton Fan Club. One fan actually wrote for a lock of my hair, so Molly cut a snippet from her black Labrador, tied a piece of ribbon to it and sent it off. The fan was delighted.

On completion of the film I flew to France to sing two Gala performances at the Casino in Deauville. At the start of my act, on the opening night, I heard angry words behind me. I had just begun to sing when a pint-sized waiter came from behind me and started to dust the top of the piano. I stopped and waited, which brought a laugh from the audience. The waiter was so nervous he only dusted half of it and scurried off. I started again, but the Maitre d'Hotel had evidently insisted the waiter dust the *other* half so he returned, which brought an even bigger laugh. The audience thought it was all part of the act.

My contract with B.I.P. gave them the right to loan me out to other studios. C. M. Woolf borrowed me for *King of the Castle* in which I starred with Hollywood's June Clyde. During the picture we became firm friends, after she had given me an embarrassing moment in the first scene of the film. We were sitting together on a garden seat when the director shouted 'Roll 'em'. This sweet, demure little blonde suddenly turned into an electric dynamo and took the scene from me. 'Cut' shouted the director. June resumed her meek pose and said to me very quietly 'Do you have much movie experience?' I hardly knew what to say. She obviously couldn't have read James Agate's praise for my performance in *Young Woodley* and other films (!!). I looked at her, liked what I saw and decided to pocket my pride. In a still quieter voice, I replied humbly 'No'. I waited for some humiliating remark. None was forthcoming. She said 'Then I will teach you', and proceeded to do so!

June, an experienced actress, had worked in Hollywood mainly for M.G.M. She had married T. Thornton Freeland, director of Fred Astaire's film *Flying down to Rio*. The Freelands kept one foot in Britain by having

[123]

an apartment in Charles Street, Mayfair; and they had another in Fort Lauderdale, Florida.

One evening over several pre-dinner cocktails with June and 'T' and their guests, film director Victor Saville and Mrs Gestetner (the 'duplicating' millionairess), I got heated when I heard wealthy Mrs G. advising June 'You can buy a loaf of bread a penny cheaper at Selfridges' bakery department'. (Incidentally, it was a fivepenny bus ride away.) She then said she would like to find something to make her feel more energetic and look younger. This remark, coming after her penny-pinching suggestion, made me sally forth with something I knew to be true. I said reprovingly, 'Beauty comes from within. If you are generous in thought, word and deed, that in itself will make you feel and look younger.'

I have a horror of meanness in any form; my little speech had left me breathless. Luckily, Victor Saville came to my rescue and endorsed my opinion. He instanced two of the most beautiful women he had met in pictures, Deborah Kerr and Greer Garson, and said 'They were generous, outgoing ladies and because of it possessed a spiritual magnetism that transmitted itself on stage and screen.' I think the point was made.

June and I were ideal as a team and *King of the Castle* made money. Redd Davis, our director, had his own peculiar brand of humour. Sometimes at the end of a scene he would wander up, pat us on the back and say 'That was good'. Then as an apparent afterthought he added 'Of course, there are two kinds of good – good for nothing and good and lousy. That was both, let's do it again'.

Claude Dampier the comedian played the role of my butler. In conversation on the first day of his filming, I asked how long his contract was for. 'Three days' he replied, and added 'But I'll be here longer than that'. I was puzzled, but soon learned the reason for his confident answer – he stretched his part. He would say a line of dialogue, then pause and say 'Y—e—s' then repeat the line and then give you the cue. The effect was funny, so they let him get away with it. In one scene he was showing me round the baronial hall of my newly-inherited castle. He came to a halt in front of a large gilt-framed painting. 'This' he proclaimed 'is your grandfather. Y—e—s. He was killed hunting, sir.' I enquired 'Where?' 'Piccadilly Circus.'

I heard later that Redd Davis went to Monte Carlo a rich man and lost every penny gambling at the Casino. The last we heard of him was that he was working as a chef on the Canadian Pacific Railway.

I grew a moustache to play a penniless continental prince in the film

Trade show poster for *King of the Castle*.

Once in a Million, with Charles 'Buddy' Rogers, who married Mary Pickford. Buddy was a kind person. I remember an occasion when a thunderstorm broke during filming. The little girl working on the set with us was very frightened. Buddy comforted her and said in his broad American accent 'Don't worry, honey, it's only the fairies moving their furniture.' Ronald Neame, who became an accomplished international director, photographed the film beautifully, while Arthur Woods got the best out of us as director.

No Exit, the next film, in which I starred with Valerie Hobson and Leslie Perrins, brought me a great deal of publicity and a narrow escape from death by suffocation when I was locked in a leather trunk. The fault was mine. I was asked whether a few holes should be punched in the trunk for ventilation and I told the director it was silly to spoil an expensive trunk for the few seconds I would be in it. The locks jammed and when eventually it was broken open, I was unconscious.

Valerie Hobson had made pictures in Hollywood and was inclined to be haughty. She kept suggesting to the director, Norman Lee, he ought to do this or ought to do that. He became so annoyed with Valerie that on one of the more difficult days, he shouted to everyone on the set 'Let's get on with Miss Hobson's scene this morning, so that we can get on with the picture this afternoon'.

Rosa Lewis, owner of the Cavendish Hotel in Jermyn Street, S.W.1. – which, it was said, was given to her by King Edward VII after a quick romp in the kitchen one hot summer's afternoon – asked me to sing at an important party she was giving for a foreign diplomat. As Rosa knew everybody who mattered, I dared not refuse. When I arrived I found the large drawing-room jammed with guests. I informed the butler I would be ready to sing whenever Miss Lewis desired. A few minutes later the butler beckoned me and I had to fight my way through the crowd to the piano. The guests wouldn't keep their conversation down, so after a few songs I gave up and fought my way out of the room again.

While I was cooling off in the corridor, Rosa appeared and said reprovingly 'So there you are, Billy. You naughty boy, we've been waiting for you. Now what are you going to sing for us?' Amazed, I replied 'But I've just sung'. 'Never mind, dear,' she chirped, and dragged me back to the piano. This time the crowd was silenced before I began. As I was singing I could not help noticing a beautiful middle-aged woman who was leaning forward on the piano. Her sex-appeal sagged where it shouldn't, but I thought she obviously had an income that hid all her

Buddy Rogers and I in a scene from *Once in a Million*.

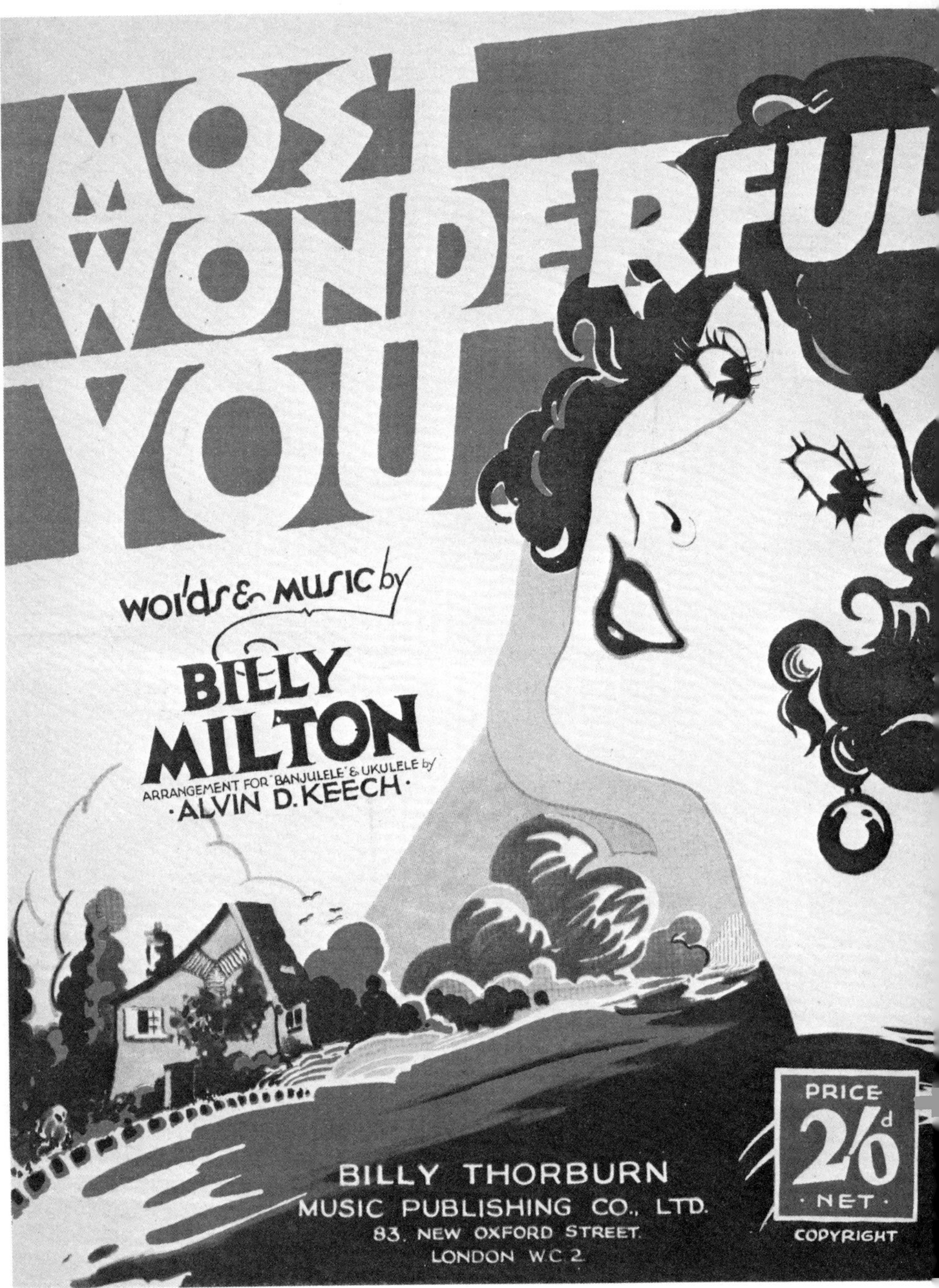

MOST WONDERFUL YOU
words & music by
BILLY MILTON
ARRANGEMENT FOR "BANJULELE" & UKULELE by
ALVIN D. KEECH
BILLY THORBURN
MUSIC PUBLISHING CO., LTD.
83, NEW OXFORD STREET
LONDON W.C.2
PRICE 2/- NET
COPYRIGHT

faults. When I asked Rosa who she was, she said 'My dear, that's Veronica. She's lived successfully off her friends for the past twenty-five years.'

Noah Beery played villain to my hero at the Elstree Studios in a screen version of the stage success, *Someone at the Door*. Watching one particular scene, I noticed Noah coughed a great deal. He would stop and ask for a glass of water. I thought he had caught a cold. But no; the truth of the matter was that Noah, playing the scene with Edward Chapman, was worried this excellent actor might steal it from him. Any time Noah felt things were not going too well for him, he started a bout of coughing which brought the proceedings to a halt, until he had the scene going the way he wanted.

Herbert Brenon, who directed, was fond of practical jokes and pulled a few tricks to soften up Chapman, a brilliant actor, but aggressive and not too popular on the set. We were working in a fumed-oak drawing-room set where Chapman had to fire a revolver. Herbert suggested he try it out to make sure it was in good working order. 'Don't point the bloody thing at the floor,' yelled Brenon, 'you might injure your foot. Point it upwards and fire,' which Chapman did, and was deluged from above with a collection of prop stuffed birds. In another scene, two suitcases were involved. Chapman, as the sinister manservant, had to open the front door and take them from Noah and me. They were actually empty. The first take was okay, but Brenon pretended he needed a re-take. This time, unbeknown to Chapman, he had the suitcases filled with lead. You can imagine the look of surprise that registered on Chapman's face when he took the (now) heavy suitcases from us and then dropped them, while Brenon fumed at him.

Herbert Brenon preferred drama and as *Someone at the Door* was a comedy-thriller, he wasn't too happy about it. He didn't like young people in general and me in particular. Early on he tried to get me replaced in the part by what appeared, at first, to be a friendly gesture. He would shout 'Roll 'em' to the camera, then approach me and give new instructions ending with the words 'Do try and remember your lines, Billy'. This puzzled me as I had not made any mistakes in the previous take. One of the cameramen tipped me off as to what he was up to. Brenon knew that everything he said was being recorded, and when the top executives saw the 'rushes' next day in the projection room, it was possible he could shake their confidence in me. From then on I refused to start any scene until Brenon was off the set and safely behind the camera.

There was another occasion when I was tied to a chair while Noah

Beery interrogated me and had to slap my face, twice. When it came to rehearsing the slaps, Noah was wearing a heavy ring which he intended to remove for the 'take', so he just went through the motions. 'No!' shouted Brenon. 'This is the way I want you to do it,' and he proceeded to knock my head nearly off my shoulders.

Brenon had gained fame in Hollywood as the only director who had ever dared throw a chair at Greta Garbo. After he made a big success with his film *Beau Geste* (in which Noah Beery played the sadistic Sergeant Lejaune) he became a real tyrant. One of his favourite ploys before a fight sequence, was to tell one actor of the derogatory remarks that another actor had made about him. The result was a great fight.

A more amusing episode was when the sound recordist asked Noah Beery to use less volume when he spoke his dialogue. Noah had been a Shakespearian actor and said, as an aside to me, 'I have a large organ'. The microphone was directly overhead, the sound man heard what he said and chipped in 'We've all heard you have, but I'm talking about your voice'.

Phillips Holmes arrived from Hollywood to join Diana Churchill and myself in *The Dominant Sex*, which, unfortunately, Herbert Brenon was also to direct. Phillips and I settled down to work without any mention of the night we had at Cold Water Canyon. Sadly, Phillips was to die young. Time tells on a man, particularly a good time.

I went straight from this movie into *A Star fell from Heaven* with Florine McKinney from Hollywood, my leading lady. There were four comedians in the cast: W. H. Berry, George Graves, Steve Geray and C. Dernier Warren. The tricks they got up to to win the honours had to be seen to be believed. They gave a tough time to the star, diminutive pocket-tenor Joseph Schmidt. He was so small that in certain scenes, he had to walk on soap-boxes laid end to end out of camera, so as to appear of normal height. Schmidt had a superb voice and his record 'My song goes round the World' still gives enormous pleasure to millions.

Spring Handicap followed, with Will Fyffe the great Scottish actor and comedian. It was a run-of-the-mill story of a horse who surprised everyone by winning an important race. It was only made memorable for me by Will Fyffe's astonishing ability to turn on the tears at any given moment.

June Clyde and I resumed our partnership again and provided the romantic interest in the film I found most enjoyable to make, *Aren't Men Beasts*. The two greats, Robertson Hare and Alfred Drayton, were direc-

Sally Gray and I in a scene from *Saturday Night Revue*.

ted by Graham Cutts and they repeated the success they had made in the original stage version at the Strand Theatre. Ruth Maitland gave excellent support as an irate wife – there was no sense of line in Ruth's general design, but her foundations were simply superb. The cameraman had trouble with Alfred Drayton who would keep up-staging 'Bunny' Hare. I found a way out of the difficulty by telling Alfred that every time he did, he went out of focus; that soon cured him.

I realised I was making too many movies, too quickly. Almost before I could get my breath back I was filming again, this time in a musical called *Saturday Night Revue*. My co-star was beautiful Sally Gray, whom I had first met when she was Connie Stevens, a very talented member of the chorus in *Bow Bells* at the Hippodrome. Stanley Lupino had great faith in Sally and helped her to stardom. I too fell in love with Sally, and gave her a gold bracelet as a memento, with the names of every show and film in which she had appeared, engraved on small gold medallions. When Stanley saw my gift, he was jealous. He firmly refused to have me in his next picture *Love Lies*, which he was to direct. When Stanley died at an early age he left £14,000 to Sally in his will. Sally Gray retired from the film world to become Lady Oranmore and Brown, and now lives in Ireland.

I was asked, yet again, to compere the Film Ball at the Royal Albert Hall, the major social event of the film world. It was a particularly glittering occasion which attracted nearly 6,000 happy film folk, with a turn-out of stars rarely witnessed previously in this country including Cary Grant, Otto Kruger, Robert Young, Buddy Rogers, Charles Laughton, Leslie Henson, Lee Tracy, Rex Harrison, June Clyde and Vivien Leigh. I presented them all just before the cabaret in which a surprise appearance was made by Gracie Fields, who received a tremendous ovation. Sally Gray and I also appeared in the cabaret and sang 'Together', the *Saturday Night Revue*'s theme song, accompanied by Billy Cotton and His Band.

Two crowded years had elapsed since I had returned from New York and I was looking forward to a third year working for the same film company, when something quite unforeseen happened. I was in the middle of *The Last Chance*, a drama with Judy Kelly and Wyndham Goldie, when we were all informed of a complete policy change at British International Pictures. No further options were to be taken up on the contracts of any artists, directors or writers. The news came so suddenly it threw me momentarily.

I remembered my father's advice. When anything bad happens, top it

with something big. So I informed the studio that I must finish filming
by 1 September as I was contracted to appear in Cabaret at the Rainbow
Room in New York. Nothing was further from the truth, but to keep up
the bluff, I booked a passage to New York on the S.S. *Normandie* and kept
my legs crossed that when I arrived there, some miracle might happen.

CHAPTER ELEVEN

Miracles Sometimes Happen

ARRIVING IN NEW YORK, I MADE MY WAY TO THE WARWICK, a hotel popular with show-biz folk. Weeks slipped by, but my agent, Richard Krakeur, couldn't find an opening for me anywhere. I was beginning to despair, when one evening I was sitting in the hotel lounge and in walked my friend Sheila Barrett, the radio comedienne. She had just finished a broadcast and had popped in for a drink with friends. Surprised, she said 'Billy, what are you doing here?' I replied honestly, 'Looking for work, Sheila'. 'I've just finished at the Rainbow Room,' she said. 'That would be a good spot for you.' 'And who's going to do something about it?' I enquired. 'I will' she said and without further ado, she called the bell-boy to bring a telegraph form.

The next morning Richard Krakeur rang to say John Roy, the manager, and John D. Rockefeller Jr., would like me to audition that afternoon at the Rainbow Room. With so little time to rehearse, I was so scared that I swallowed a couple of calming pills. When the audition was over, John Roy said 'Mr Milton, if you had tried to over-sell your act, we wouldn't consider you, but you were so nonchalant, so English, we are sure you are just right for our room. We can offer you a season in February'. Richard Krakeur accepted with alacrity. It was then late October and as I had already been in New York for a couple of months, I decided to return home and find new material. I booked a passage in the S.S. *Ile de France*.

Back in London, I was often stopped in the street by well-wishers who congratulated me on my New York engagement. I had forgotten I'd told them two months before that I was off to New York to play the Rainbow Room. In those days, as communications were not so easy, they thought my coming February engagement was a 'return-date' and I didn't disillusion them.

Meanwhile, Norman Marshall invited me to join Hermione Gingold in an intimate revue called *Members Only*, at the Gate Theatre in the Strand with William Chappell directing. It was fun working with Gingold, that high-priestess of low-camp with the 'Grand Dame' manner that cloaks the deadly delivery of sledge-hammer comedy. She arrived at the first rehearsal looking as though she had just come back from a holiday in some old Viennese Schloss and had no time to change from the bombazine gown with the tea rose, into something loose and fulfilling.

During one break from rehearsal we lunched with one of her admirers from the City, at the Ivy Restaurant. 'Ging' was wearing a smart black frock and a transparent black-net hat with a broad wire brim, that wobbled every time she turned her head. The host offered me a cigar which I declined, and the waiter was withdrawing when, after a surreptitious wink to me, Gingold's voice boomed 'And why haven't you offered me a cigar?'

In those days, it was not done for women to smoke cigars in public and it threw our host into a panic. The sight of 'Ging' puffing away on the largest cigar she could select was unforgettable. She looked for all the world like one of those Mona Lisa posters one sees in the Underground which some schoolboy has desecrated by drawing in a hat and a fat cigar between her lips.

Working with Gingold is a theatrical education for anyone. I shall always remember her story of the young man of uncertain sex who, looking at a Brigadier General with his leather boots, shiny sword and bristling moustache, said 'Thank heavens I'm normal'. *Members Only* kept me busy until it was time to return to New York.

The Rainbow Room was situated on the sixty-fifth floor of the Rockefeller Building and gave a wonderful panoramic view of the great metropolis. The artists made their entrance down a double-staircase, at the foot of which was the orchestra. At the touch of a button, the dance-floor revolved and brought the piano (mounted on a rostrum) in front of the bandstand. All these movements were synchronised to coincide with my entrance music. The lighting and sound equipment were the ultimate

Performing in the Rainbow Room in New York.

in quality and theatrical efficiency. Alas, my first performance was a flop.

The management had insisted I open at the 10.00 p.m. dinner show. The large room was only sparsely filled with people, who were more interested in eating than listening. It was a shattering experience. Dejectedly, I left the building and took a taxi back to my hotel. After removing my white tie and tails, I lay on the bed and wept. I felt better for it. I wondered why I had come all this way to make a fool of myself, but was thankful the press weren't there to witness the lukewarm reception I received. John Roy later told me that he never invited the press for the first three days of a show. After that, the artists had become acclimatised to the room. I wish he'd told me sooner. For the midnight show, I went straight to my dressing room without bothering to see whether it was a good house or not. When I heard my entrance music, I stepped into the limelight at the top of the stairs and as I walked down, I could see that the room was packed and the atmosphere electric. The prayer I had said in the quiet of my hotel room had been answered.

Marlene Dietrich had a party, so had Cole Porter, Ethel Merman, June Clyde and her husband. Prince George Galitzine was with Clifton Webb and his mother. Gertrude Lawrence was accompanied by Richard Rogers. With so many celebrities present, how could I go wrong? I felt on top of the world and worked that way. A fabulous night that will always remain in my memory.

The next day, happy as a bird, I revisited some of my old haunts to revive memories of the time when I was previously in New York, playing in *This Year of Grace* at the Selwyn Theatre. Greenwich Village had changed: where was Kelly's? It was there I heard for the first time 'The Man on the Flying Trapeze' and saw Freddie Carpenter and partner do their 'Collegiate Dance'. Then I had a drink at the Algonquin Hotel, famous for its Round Table Luncheons, where I met the theatrical and literary giants of the day who gathered to eat and talk. To lunch at Sardi's, the famous theatrical rendezvous, where they seemed pleased to greet the young Englishman who had done so well at the Selwyn Theatre.

I also recalled the night Noël Coward took me to a party given by Max Ewing the socialite song-writer, who had a large studio in Greenwich Village. Max's great friend was Robert Chandler the artist who, using only his thumbs, painted the most fantastic pictures. Chandler had been declared insane in every state in America, except the State of New York. He gained notoriety when he married (for one night only and the sum of $10,000) the beautiful opera star Lina Cavalieri.

In Greenwich Village one weekend, while I was appearing in the
Rainbow Room.

Max showed me a collection of photographs which covered the entire walls of one room, depicting famous people in unconventional poses and attire. There was one of the then Prince of Wales, dressed as a woman. Another of H.R.H. being lathered with soap as he crossed the line at the equator, aboard ship. But it was mostly sick material, including a picture of a hermaphrodite from a Broadway Flea Circus, who had a sex-change and sired four children.

There were quite a few odd-ball characters at the party and at about 2.00 in the morning I'd had enough and was about to leave quietly, when our host suddenly called for silence. He announced that this was to be his *last* party; he was tired of living. I thought he was drunk or joking and took no notice. But on reading my morning newspaper I was shocked to see the headline 'Max Ewing commits suicide by jumping into the Hudson River'. He was dressed in top-hat, white tie and tails, and he had affixed two weighted suitcases to his wrists.

The opening night of the Metropolitan Opera House season provided the Rainbow Room with excitement. After their show, most of the opera stars and their friends came on to celebrate. They talked incessantly in many different foreign languages. They had no intention of listening to me. They could hardly be blamed. How could they understand the English humour of my act? But the regular patrons became restless and shushed the opera stars and their friends, who in turn shushed back – it was a lively evening.

In a telegram from England came an offer to play in the film version of the Hippodrome stage success, *Yes Madam*. The salary was too good to refuse and, at the conclusion of my highly successful season at the Rainbow Room, I sailed to England on the S.S. *Ile de France*.

On the way to the docks, I said to the cab-driver 'I've a feeling I shall never see New York again'. It was 1937.

CHAPTER TWELVE

Into War

Yes *Madam*, DIRECTED BY NORMAN LEE, WAS AN AMUSING FARCE, with songs. Bobby Howes, a clever comedian, preferred to learn his words after he went on to the studio floor. It was commonplace for him to have twenty takes for one scene. This added time and expense to the picture. Bobby also wasted time entertaining the studio crew with his party-piece, 'The Whistling Sailor'. For this he painted eyebrows (with grease-paint) over his nipples, and a mouth round his navel. By expanding and contracting his stomach muscles he was able to make it look as though his navel was actually whistling! All this time-wasting had serious repercussions on his later career.

On Sundays during this period, I compered and sang on 'The Horlicks Picture House Hour' on Radio Luxemburg. I then returned to the stage in a farce by Vernon Sylvaine called *Worth a Million*. The storyline was unusual: a young man whose luck was so consistently bad, was set up in business by gangsters as Jinx Ltd. Edmund Gwenn and Claude Hulbert played the leading roles, supported by myself and Ruby Miller, the ex-Gaiety Girl of whom it was said that so many of her admirers had drunk champagne out of her slipper, that she suffered permanently from cramp in the feet. Ruby once gave me some very good advice. 'Darling, if you ever decide to give up acting, do remember there are two things out of which you can always make money – men's insides and women's outsides.'

Programme for a gala night at the Mayfair Hotel, London, in which I performed.

[141]

News of the World impressions of *Worth a Million*.

Edmund Gwenn admitted to me that he found it galling to return to his own country after his success in Hollywood, to work as stooge to Claude Hulbert. After several successful weeks in the provinces, we opened at the Saville Theatre for a West End Season. Press notices were only lukewarm. We closed after three months, which was the usual run in those days, for a flop.

During the show I was offered a large fee to sing to thirty thousand people at the East Ham Speedway. When I arrived and saw the small rostrum standing in the middle of the vast stadium, my knees shook and I began to regret having accepted the job. I had rehearsed at my studio with the sextet booked to accompany me, and left the presentation and amplification arrangements to the organisers. When I stepped into the limelight and started the long walk to the rostrum, it seemed a million miles away – it was also cold and windy. After the band had played the introduction, I began to sing a medley of popular songs, when a gust of wind blew all the music off their stands. The crowd laughed. I couldn't get going again until the music had been gathered up, sorted out and replaced. Thank goodness, when I started again the crowd joined in, always lagging a couple of bars behind!

Chili Bouchier, the film star and my sister-in-law, then asked me to join her repertory company for a season at the Ilford Hippodrome. I thought it would keep me in good theatrical trim. In H. M. Harwood's *The Man in Possession*, my role was Raymond Dabney. I carried most of the play, but it was easier for me when we produced Michael Egan's *The Dominant Sex*. I played my original screen role. Afterwards I took a well-needed rest with friends at their home in the country, little realising war was nearly upon us.

B.B.C. Radio offered me the part of The Arrow in a new drama series called 'Meet the Arrow, the Whistling Detective'. It caught on in a big way, playing to an air-audience of over six million. A troop of boy scouts in Blackpool requested permission to call themselves 'The Blackpool Arrows'.

With things going well and the prospects of a long-running and highly successful series in view, Neville Chamberlain spoke the fatal words, after first waving a bit of paper, 'We are at war with Germany'. Theatres closed, radio entertainment dispersed and was broadcast from hastily organised temporary studios in provincial towns.

While awaiting my call-up to the forces, I filled in with other radio shows, 'Waiting for Jane' and 'Monday Night at Eight', and did as many troop shows as possible. I joined Jack Buchanan's company to entertain the Guards Regiment at Victoria Barracks, Windsor, who were leaving the next day for France. The atmosphere was so tense, I went out for as many laughs as I could with lively stories, and songs in which they could all join in the chorus. They especially enjoyed my story of the two officers on leave who were having a night out at a cabaret. Seeing a bald-headed man of sixty sitting with a beautiful young girl, they sent him a note. 'Dear Professor, we are two officers on leave, may we dance with your daughter?' Back came the reply 'I am *not* a professor and this is *not* my daughter. I am an ornithological taxidermist and I intend to stuff this bird myself.' I finished with a song they enjoyed singing – 'Rattle your Bottles in Rollocks Yard'.

Collie Knox, famed critic of the *Daily Mail*, reported a typical forces show we gave during the early weeks of the war. Headed 'Stars for the Troops', it ran , ' "It would cost me thousands of pounds to put on a show like this in peacetime," remarked a famous theatrical manager during this week's big concert for the Anti-Aircraft and Balloon Barrage units. All had given their services free and as each turn in the three-hour programme was a famous star, no one minded when they went on in a show cleverly compered by Billy Milton.'

Beatrice Lillie sang of Hitler's secret weapon, Lea Seidl sang of the White Horse Inn and Douglas Byng appeared as Flora Macdonald. Edythe Baker, the diminutive American pianist, cheerfully put up with a small upright piano, but found she could not reach the keyboard because the piano stool was too low. She asked me for a cushion. There wasn't one, so as it was a matter of urgency, I took Bea Lillie's mink coat which was lying across a chair, and doubled it up for Edythe to sit on. You can imagine Bea's reaction later. Dorothy Ward, the famous Principal Boy, lured a much-medalled Brigadier on to the stage, and sang a love-duet with him while the men yelled their heads off. She really did make a meal of the poor man, sat on his knee and covered his face with bright red lipstick kisses. The press, eager for something out of the ordinary, published the pictures next day and a harmless bit of fun finished up with severe reprimands from higher-ups on both sides, military and theatrical.

A few days later, the *Star* reported, 'Three thousand members of the fighting services were entertained by West End artists somewhere-in-England. The entire show was organised and compered by Billy Milton, who took his troupe down by bus in the black-out. Among the stars who

COMBERMERE BARRACKS
WINDSOR
WEDNESDAY, NOVEMBER 22nd
Commencing at 6.15 p.m.

More November
NONSENSE

Presented by LEON CASSEL-GERARD with

JANE CARR & MARIANNE DAVIS
The West End's Favourite Cabaret Stars.

BILLY MILTON
Stage, Screen and Radio Star.

GABRIELLE BRUNE
From the Gate Revue.

GEORGE MELACHRINO
Your Favourite Singer of Songs.

TIM CLAYTON
AND
THE "FOUR HUNDRED" BAND

ALL OTHER RANKS, THEIR WIVES AND CHILDREN OVER THE AGE OF 10, ADMITTED FREE.

LUFF & SONS LTD. PRINTERS, WINDSOR

Poster for *More November Nonsense*, a show for the troops at Windsor in which I appeared.

Broadcasting 'I Found Romance . . .', a series in which I reminisced about Paris, New York, Hollywood and London with records.
[BBC COPYRIGHT PHOTOGRAPH]

gave their services free were Lea Seidl, Inga Anderson, Edythe Baker and Annette Mills, who wrote "Boomps-a-Daisy". Miss Mills brought men to the stage to dance with her and introduced her latest song, "Please Leave My Butter Alone!"' Actually, this *Celebrity Revue* was staged at Elstree Studios and took place in a French courtyard, the remains of an old film set in the B.I.P. studio. The audience were officers and men of the Royal Air Force and the Honourable Artillery Company. Artists not mentioned in the *Star* report, but a great success in the show, were Douglas Byng, The Carlyle Cousins and Happy Blake and His Coloured Orchestra.

The B.B.C. invited me to play the star role in a new series called 'Waiting for Jane'. It clicked right away and attracted a listening audience of millions. In the thirty-eighth week of its run, it had to come to an end because I received my calling-up papers.

Milton, William Thomas, signed on at Bristol and became AC2 1143340 of the Royal Air Force posted to Padgate in Lancashire for square-bashing. The day I arrived, I was ordered to report to the entertainments officer, who promptly gave me a midnight pass. This puzzled me. I was told it was his wife's birthday and he wanted me to play the piano at a party being given at his house just outside the camp. My hut mates didn't like this favouritism and gave me the cold shoulder. I got back into their good books when I agreed to compose love letters for them which they could copy and send to their sweethearts and wives. They evidently thought that with my worldly experience I had a better technique.

Tough sergeants abounded at Padgate. One was particularly sadistic. I felt sorry for some of the country lads on whom he vented his venom. He had a face like a knee-cap and I was never sure whether he was smiling at me or just baring his teeth. His dislike of me was instant and complete and he laid many snares to trap me into insubordination. But I was a little too experienced to fall for that sort of nonsense. His favourite ploy was to address me in a la-de-dah voice, taking the mickey in the hope I would retaliate. Typical was his demonstration of handling weapons. Ignoring the rest of the squad, he addressed me directly. 'The term firearm, my pretty little dancing elf, is a generic designation of weapons which throw a missile by virtue of the propellant power generated by a charge of suitable explosive. Do you get that, Milton?' Innocently, I replied 'Not quite, sergeant. Would you please repeat it for me?'

The entertainments officer ordered me to volunteer to compere the shows given in the gymnasium for troops who had completed their

Tommy Linden as he appeared in *Strike a New Note*.

training and were being 'passed out'. I was quite happy to do it as it brought me a few 'excused-duty' perks and gave me a chance to do something more useful than learning how to march up and down a parade ground. My long professional experience enabled me to hold a tough two-thousand strong male audience. After a number of these concerts, I was told to report to the C.O. who instructed me to go to Drury Lane Theatre (complete with Pass and Travel Warrant) for an interview with Sir Seymour Hicks.

AC2 Milton, 1143340, obeyed orders and was duly seconded by Sir Seymour to ENSA and told to form his own company. The first was *The Service Revue*, produced by Archie de Bear, originator of the *Co-optimists*. We travelled the country promoting goodwill in British and American camps, but in Ireland our company manager once had difficulty with some randy American troops who wanted to rape our girls. They were dressing behind screens in the canteen kitchen, because there was no other accommodation.

As well as the happy days there were sad moments. I recall the time I was having a before-the-show drink with some young R.A.F. pilots at an air base in Norfolk The alert sounded, they quickly scrambled and took off on a mission over Holland. The Germans were waiting for them, and only a handful returned. The padre asked me to go to the mess as quickly as possible after the show and play the piano; he thought it might help. I felt it was pitifully inadequate.

Doing the rounds of the camps and H.Q.s I met professional people who were surprised I was traipsing around entertaining as a humble AC2. The next thing I knew I was being told to report for an interview at the R.A.F. H.Q., Adastra House in London. I was taken in front of a high-ranking officer who had so much 'egg' on his hat, I could have easily made an omelette. He said airily 'A star of your standing should be commissioned as an officer'. I thanked him but politely declined his suggestion. There were times when I regretted my hasty decision to stay in the ranks, but I think the truth was I enjoyed being there. I stayed AC2 throughout my service in the R.A.F.

When playing the Dover area, I had a couple of narrow squeaks. The Flying V Bombs came over regularly on their way to London. Our pilots endeavoured to explode them over the sea. On one occasion when bathing, I had to take cover by a breakwater because shrapnel and pieces of bomb were splattering around. One evening I was sitting at the dressing-table, making-up for the show. As I leaned forward to look closer in the mirror – wham! – a piece of shrapnel embedded itself in the wood of the mirror. If I hadn't moved forward at that moment, it would have taken my head off. Meat pies became my staple diet as we toured the camps. I'm sure that every time we passed a horse, it bowed to me.

Anna Neagle and Herbert Wilcox invited me to join their new ENSA company. Frank Collins, who at that time was connected with Drury Lane ENSA units, gloomily predicted that Anna was too lightweight and would never go down with the troops. How wrong he was: Anna was a riot. Her warmth and charm, especially in her 'Alice Blue Gown' number, delighted them. She wore a red wig which off-set her stunning blue gown and she looked a dream. In her autobiography *There's Always Tomorrow*, Anna wrote 'Billy Milton kept things going with his songs and light-hearted patter. He seemed to know just how to adapt himself to each and every audience.'

After approximately two thousand shows for the troops, AC2 1143340, Milton, collapsed and was ordered to rest for three months, before being honourably discharged from the R.A.F.

I rented a flat above the Savoy Turkish Baths in Jermyn Street, Piccadilly, which I shared with Tommy Linden, the South African dancer and choreographer. Tommy made a big hit in the revue *Strike a New Note* at the Prince of Wales Theatre, with comedian Sid Field. Years later, after being told by a thoughtless B.B.C. producer that his choreography had become old fashioned (a soul-destroying thing to say to any sensitive artist), Tommy went to Portugal where, sadly, he took his own life.

I have memories of a similar occurrence when I lived in Hollywood. The American lyric writer Roy Turk, who wrote some of Bing Crosby's world hits, was told by M.G.M. Studios that his lyrics were old-fashioned, which he took to mean that he was through. That afternoon he stumbled into my bungalow at the Garden of Allah, absolutely stunned. He finally broke down and wept. How can anyone, with so much experience and success behind them, suddenly cease to have any talent? Roy's death was hastened by this unhappy incident – and to think his songs are still bringing in a mint of royalties today.

David Niven crossed my path again in an amusing manner, but this time in England. I was filming at Elstree and came home early one evening and saw that the portrait of me painted by Frank Slater, which hung over the fireplace, was missing. I asked Tommy where it was. He replied 'I got fed-up with looking at it, so I put it in the box-room'. I laughed and said 'Okay, I'll get a mirror to replace it, but in the meantime,

The vanishing portrait, below; it shows me in *Bitter Sweet*. The portrait above shows me as Dame Sarah in *Dick Whittington*, of which more later.

[151]

put the picture back as it has left a dirty mark'. A week later, the same thing happened again. This time I was annoyed and got the truth. Tommy had remembered my story of how I first met Niven in Hollywood. Wanting to give the impression the flat was his, he removed my picture every time Niven called.

Tommy Linden was a great admirer of David Niven, especially his elegant voice. An actor, who bore me a grudge (I never discovered why), was determined to break up the friendship between Tommy and me. His plan was exceedingly cunning. When he knew I would be otherwise engaged, he invited Tommy to a late-night party. During the evening he bet Tommy a fiver he would not be able to identify the owner of the voice that would speak to him out of the total darkness of the next room. To his delight Tommy recognised it straight away and that was the beginning of the slow goodbye. As the song says 'Breaking up is so hard to Do'. I moved from our flat to the Pastoria Hotel, off Leicester Square.

I was Frank Slater's first model, his original guinea-pig long before he rose to fame as a highly successful portrait painter. I used to sit for him in his cold and draughty studio at Notting Hill Gate. The place was only partially heated by one of those large, ungainly stoves that emit revolting smells. By way of thanks, he promised to paint my portrait every ten years. This he did. Success took him from that Notting Hill Gate room to a large house in Edwardes Square, W.8. Then, with commissions pouring in, he moved to New York and international fame. Because of pressure of work and his enormous appetite for the fair sex, he died quite young.

Early one morning, I heard a repeated knocking on the door of our flat. At that hour (it was almost the crack of noon), I thought it must surely be the police. In my dressing gown, I half-opened the door and saw the famous impresario, Emile Littler. He explained he wanted me to play Jimmy Bronson in his revival of *The Belle of New York* at the London Coliseum. What a time to tell me, I hadn't even had my morning cup of gin! Correspondence was subsequently exchanged, then I heard no more. I thought 'Oh well, he's had second thoughts'. And he had! Shortly afterwards, Audrey Thacker, my agent, told me Emile now wanted me to play 'Tony Chute' in the revival of *The Quaker Girl*.

CHAPTER THIRTEEN

An Affair with a Quaker Girl

JESSIE MATTHEWS WAS TO PLAY THE TITLE ROLE. I HAD AN AWKward moment when, dressed in my best suit, I met her in Emile's office. The first thing she said was 'Emile, I think Billy is a bit short for me'. I could see my big chance going out of the window, so I said quickly 'Jessie, take your shoes off. No Quaker Girl wears high heels.' That saved me.

When rehearsals started I soon realised the show was saddled with three producers: Emile Littler, Major Freddie Lloyd and Vernon Sylvaine. The version of *Quaker Girl* varied with whoever was taking rehearsal. I played it safe and listened to Major Lloyd who knew the show backwards, and knew where the laughs were. Hal Bryan was Jerimiah, Geoffrey Dunn played the Prince and Ivy St. Helier was Madame Blum. I used to see Miss St. Helier busily advising Jessie where she should be in each scene. 'This is strange' I thought, because Miss St. Helier was a friend of Evelyn Laye, from whom Jessie had annexed (and later married) her husband, Sonnie Hale. Some of her advice seemed to suggest that Jessie was being incorrectly produced. This had an unsettling effect on her.

Betty Robb the pianist and I were asked by Emile to go one Sunday to Jessie's house at Old Hampton, to run through the songs with her. At one point Jessie stopped, went over to the sofa and lay down full length on it. She then put a square of black velvet over her eyes and after a few moments, told us that her spirit guide was talking to her. She asked for a pencil and paper and wrote down a poem which she later read to us. The whole incident was odd and rather mystifying.

Next day we rehearsed the scene in which I was to give the Quaker Girl her first dancing lesson. The rehearsal was private, the only people on stage were Jessie, myself and the ballet-mistress, Phyl Blakeston. Jessie's conception of the dance was bewildering. I quite understood her desire to display her dancing talent, but this was supposed to be her first lesson in dancing. The steps Jessie suggested and wanted to rehearse were these (they will ever remain indelible in my memory): 'Sway left – sway right – a round kick from her – then four quick pirouettes to the right – stop and then repeat'. I thought it completely out of place for a beginner learning to dance. For the sake of discretion, I said nothing. However I did notice that the ballet mistress had disappeared. Presumably she had gone to report to Emile.

I was excused rehearsal next day as I was contracted to do a broadcast, so I was absent when Jessie and Emile had a confrontation. It was a row that led to headlines in the *Evening News* which read 'Jessie Matthews quits Quaker Girl Coliseum show'. It transpired that Jessie had told Bill Bourne, one of the kindest of theatrical journalists, her side of the story. I thought this action was foolish and could do her harm.

When I arrived at the theatre next day I was told to report to Emile's office. Rehearsals were at a standstill and I wondered how it was going to affect me. Then Emile told me his side of the story. It was obvious that something had to be done quickly about finding a replacement. I phoned Jack Fallon (my agent in the Jack Hylton office) and told him about a girl I had seen playing in pantomime at the King's Theatre, Hammersmith, the previous night. I went there on the recommendation of Betty Robb, and at the first interval went backstage to see the girl – Celia Lipton, daughter of West End band-leader Sidney Lipton. I introduced myself, congratulated her on the performance and asked for a photograph. She said (rather grandly, I thought), 'Come round after the show'. I thought 'To hell with that, I've got a supper date'. But the powers-that-be were told, and within hours Celia Lipton was in Emile's office and ten days later, we opened successfully at the Coventry Hippodrome, prior to opening in London. At our last run-through on the morning of our Coventry opening, I remember Emile saying one thing in particular which was a shock to us all, 'I should have produced this by a river so I could have thrown myself in!'

[154]

A sketch by 'Tom Titt' of Celia Lipton and me dancing in *The Quaker Girl*.

During the opening performance that night, a short while before I was to make my entrance to play a love scene with the Quaker Girl (which was full of 'thee's' and 'thou's') Emile burst through the pass-door and started to give me notes on my performance. Upset, I said 'Emile, will you kindly leave me alone. I've already walked the streets of Coventry trying to forget some of the things you said to us this morning.' At the end of the first act, I was in my dressing room busily changing, when Emile came in. Dreading more notes and despite my being only half-dressed, I took flight to the men's toilet upstairs, locked myself in and refused to budge until he had left my room. Only when my dresser had assured me that Emile had gone, would I come down.

The first night was a triumph and we played to capacity business right through the week. A couple of nights later, just before the curtain was due to go up, I was on stage warming-up with a few dance-steps when Emile emerged from the shadows. He put his hand on my shoulder and said 'Here are some gags for you, Billy, put them in and I'll tell you what you can keep. I didn't know you were so temperamental.' I replied 'I'm not, Emile, but you give me a wonderful part, a good salary and then you nearly ruin it by giving me your notes in the middle of a first night performance when I was overwrought with nerves.'

The London Coliseum production was delightful, with Dorothy Zinkeisen's sets and costumes and Michael Collins conducting an augmented orchestra. Celia Lipton and I made a perfect team. We never had a cross word the whole time we worked together. However, looking into my tiny jewel-box of memories, there was one big disappointment. After our London opening Emile gave a first-night party at the Savoy Hotel Grill. Jack Hylton was disgusted when he learned that I had not been invited. He considered my contribution to the show warranted more gracious treatment. Incensed, Jack booked a table for his wife Fifi Hylton, Teddy Knox and myself, next to the Littler table and insisted I do exactly as he instructed. When he gave me the signal, I was to rise and toast Celia first, then later rise and toast Emile and finally Sidney Lipton. I duly obeyed Jack's instructions and I am sure the point was made!

We played four matinées a week at the Coliseum, also nightly at 6.30 p.m. and, because the bombs were falling on London, I fire-watched as well, sleeping in my dressing-room if I couldn't get home. Sometimes during a performance a bomb would fall close by and the whole theatre shook. Dust would descend slowly from the dome into the limelight, giving an eerie effect. But we carried on and occasionally there was a line

On the road with *Blue for a Boy*, left to right: two friends, Joan Emney, Burt Brownhill, Martin Tiffin and me.

in the dialogue which the audience could relate to the raid in progress and it would get a big laugh.

The road opposite the stage-door led to the Strand and Charing Cross Station. It was a popular 'hen-run'. One regular was perambulating one evening in the blackout, when she saw on the other side of the road, the manly back of a possible client. She crossed and found he was a man of the cloth. Smiling sweetly she said, 'Good evening vicar. What's it going to be, "Onward Christian Soldiers" or "Abide with Me"?'

We opened at the London Coliseum on 23 May 1944. A few months later the bombs finally drove us out on tour. During a matinée at the Opera House in Blackpool, the stage-door keeper came to my dressing room and said 'Mr Milton, there's a crowd outside demanding to see you. People can't pass on the pavement and the police are complaining.' It was during the third act and I was in full evening dress. As I stepped out into the bright sunshine in full make-up, I felt an idiot when I saw it was a large troupe of Boy and Girl Scouts. They were waving banners on which was emblazoned THE BLACKPOOL ARROWS. They were my 'Meet the Arrow' radio fans who had come to invite me to go under canvas with them. As there wasn't time to do that I promised I would have tea with them instead!

After a long provincial tour we returned to London in February 1945, to open at the Stoll Theatre in Kingsway. After a lengthy stay there we went out on another tour and finally *The Quaker Girl* came to rest in December 1948, four and a half years after our opening at the London Coliseum. I shall always remember Hal Bryan, the comedian playing the role of Jerimiah, got a big laugh at every performance with some lines that are still appropriate today. 'A stockbroker is a man who buys something he can't get, with money he hasn't got. Then he sells what he never had, for more than it ever cost. It's all governed by what they call boom and slump.'

Tip Toes, a musical comedy with a George Gershwin score and presented by J. P. Sherwood, was my next show. Natasha Sokolova, beautiful daughter of ballerina Lydia Sokolova, was to be my leading lady. Natasha was primarily a dancer and had never before sung in musicals. As we rehearsed the hit number 'That certain Feeling', I realised her tiny voice was rapidly vanishing with the strain. For the sake of the show and the approaching first night, I secretly rehearsed with her understudy when everyone left. Came the opening night and, as I feared, Natasha was voiceless. The curtain went up with a newcomer in the leading role and the

Burt Brownhill, Martin Tiffin and I in a scene from *Blue for a Boy*.

A scene from *Blue for a Boy*: Leonora Walsh, me and the chorus.

press acclaimed a new starlet, Mary Meredith.

After the run of *Tip Toes*, Emile Littler asked me to do yet another tour of *The Quaker Girl*, but this time with a salary cut. As I had nothing in view and it was a good part, I accepted. The week we played Plymouth, Emile phoned for me to see him immediately. I travelled overnight after the show, to London. He wanted me to play in an American musical, *The Red Mill*. The idea was to run it in for fourteen weeks on tour and then present it at the Palace Theatre, London. When I asked if I might read the script and hear the music, he said neither was available. I got up and walked to the door. 'Where are you going?' he asked. I replied 'You surely don't expect me to accept a part, unseen?' He said firmly 'I want you to do it'. His manner and intention seemed to indicate that if I refused, it could mean a loss of work. Foolishly I gave in and agreed. *The Red Mill* toured for fourteen weeks, but in my opinion it was one of those American shows that didn't survive the Atlantic crossing. I breathed a sigh of relief when at last the 'notice to close' went up on the board at the King's Theatre, Glasgow. 'Thank goodness that's over' I thought.

To my amazement Emile re-cast the show and brought in the famous music hall comedians Jewel and Warris to replace myself and American comedian Slim Allen. *The Red Mill* opened at the Palace – then closed after the first night! Emile asked me to go out again with *The Quaker Girl*, again at a cut in salary. I refused.

By some strange coincidence I found theatrical work was a little more difficult to get. Thank goodness plenty of radio work came in and enabled me to carry on quite nicely, financially. Then, quite out of the blue eighteen months later, came a request for me to audition for a leading role in a number one tour of Emile Littler's musical *Blue for a Boy*. That I was asked to audition after having worked so long for Littler was humiliating, but the salary offered was even more so. I had learned the hard way that it is sometimes unwise to stand up for fair play in the theatre so, in the financial circumstances, I had to accept.

Blue for a Boy had run successfully for two years at Her Majesty's Theatre with Fred Emney and Richard Hearne, but I felt the touring cast was stronger. Comedians Bert Brownhill and Martin Tiffen were superb and we kept the show moving at a brisk pace. The leading lady was Beryl Seaton, who was later to lead in *Finian's Rainbow* at the Palace Theatre. Joan Emney, Fred's sister, and Leonora Walsh provided the feminine interest. We ran for nearly a year with great success

Although we played all round the British Isles, I still managed to do quite a bit of radio work. It often entailed some extraordinary journeys. Typical was the one I made when playing at the Pavilion, Torquay. A local newspaper reported 'To appear in the Light Programme show "Up and Coming" (production by Trafford Whitelock), Billy Milton leaves Torquay at 12.05 in the morning, arrives in London at 7.25 a.m., goes straight to rehearsal at the Paris Cinema, is on the air from 12.25 to 12.55 and catches the 1.30 p.m. train back to Torquay, due to arrive just in time for the curtain of *Blue for a Boy*.' Thank goodness in those days, railway management and men were at peace and trains were punctual!

CHAPTER FOURTEEN

A Dream comes True

AT A PARTY IN THE KING'S ROAD, CHELSEA, I WAS TALKING TO
Emlyn Williams when a tall, distinguished-looking man walked over to
see me and said 'You're Billy Milton, you know about revue'. Surprised,
I answered, 'Well, I've appeared in a few in London, Paris and New
York . . .' and before I could continue, he said 'Direct one for me. I'm
John Wyse, my partner and I run the Bolton's Theatre – we want it in
four weeks.' I thought that he must be joking as they only put on plays at
the Bolton's. Early next morning my phone rang; it was John Wyse.
'What are you doing about our revue?' We met, the contract was fixed
and the fulfilment of my schoolboy dream had come true.

Material was one of the first priorities, so I contacted top composers
and lyric writers – Eric Maschwitz, Jack Strachey, Michael Treford and
Alfred Shaughnessy – also pianists Kenneth Broadberry and Robb
Stewart. Daphne Anderson was my choice for leading lady, clever,
versatile and maid of all work. Comedian Reg Varney I found doing a
troop show at the Café de Paris. I was impressed by his act and we talked
after the show. I explained to him that because of the small capacity (just
over 150 seats) and the theatre's financial position each member of the
cast (including myself) would receive £3.10/– a week, but it would
provide a marvellous shop window. To my delight he agreed. Richard
Gilbert, a tall, elegant young man, came to the audition in a taxi which he

could ill afford and had us in stitches with his hilarious description of the Royal Wedding. He was a 'must' because he made a sharp contrast to the cockney-accented Varney. Red-headed Rosaline Hadden, Cicely Court-neidge's tall and shy niece, sang of the woes of a girl who was 'too tall', whilst Sheila Matthews and Patricia Dainton sang and danced enchantingly. Donald Reed, the choreographer, excelled himself as the smug peer 'Little Lord Fauntleroy – who little girls seemed to annoy'. I had a number 'No Orchids for my Lady' which was later recorded by Frank Sinatra. Michael Treford, who wrote one of Eartha Kitt's biggest hits 'An Englishman needs Time', contributed some lyrical gems, and Geoffrey Ghin got his first big break as a designer with his scenery and costumes for the show.

Unfortunately the financial reserves of this courageous theatre were low, but John Wyse had faith in me to restore them and allowed me to do things that were unconventional. My first instruction to the box-office was to inform those members who had left their booking to the last minute, that the house was sold out for the first two performances. It caused a lot of talk, and in any case we could fill the house with friends and relatives of the cast. Good publicity at no cost!

To get extra press coverage, I rashly decided to drive a coach-and-four, laden with members of the company, around Piccadilly Circus, Shaftesbury Avenue and Leicester Square. All went well until a car back-fired and the horses took off. I went to bed that night with arms that felt six feet long from my efforts to control the brutes! I also altered the usual seating arrangements for the newspaper critics and put most of them in a row which Reg Varney used during a sketch he played in the auditorium. The tricks worked well. When I opened the morning papers after the first night, the headlines read 'Great little revue' and reports described Reg Varney as a 'comic genius'. I knew we were home and dry. W. A. Darlington, Harold Hobson, Peter Black, Alan Dent, Kenneth A. Hurren and Bill Bourne, the country's most distinguished critics, did us proud. The box-office telephones rang continuously and we played to capacity standing-room-only business every performance.

Queen Mary honoured us by coming to the show. How *Bolton's Revue* came to her notice will ever remain a mystery for me. I received a message from her Lady-in-Waiting that nothing was to be altered because of Her Majesty's visit. Queen Mary particularly liked the comedy number I sang 'I'm the only Fakir on the Pier'. The solitary prop on the stage was a large box, decorated in the same fashion as a Fortune-Teller machine on a seaside Pier. I was concealed inside, with only my head (and ornate turban) protruding through the hole at the top. The song told of the chagrin of a mechanical fortune-teller whose predictions were automatically delivered by the insertion of a coin in the machine. In the lyric the accent falls on the first syllable of 'Fakir', which is pronounced 'Farkeer'.

I'M THE ONLY FAKIR ON THE PIER
Michael Treford and Billy Milton

I'm the only Fakir on the Pier
And it's hardly the place for a seer, here
Far away from the comforts of tropical Ind
You don't know how I suffer from the cold and the wind
And it's very bad luck when my drawers get stuck
And the rabble starts shaking them clear
They bang on my sides at the slightest suggestion
And they leave my integrity open to question
And their bent pennies give me such acute indigestion
To the only Fakir on the Pier.

I'm the only Fakir on the Pier
And I really must shed an austere tear
In winter, by frost's icy fingers I'm gripped
Why even brass monkeys are better equipped
And then little boys write on my sides with delight
Words not even used in Kashmir
I contemplate much though I don't want to boast
In a yoga-like trance I'm often engrossed
But the paint's wearing off where I contemplate most
I'm the only Fakir on the Pier.

I'm the only Fakir on the Pier
And sometimes I feel ever so queer, dear
The trippers don't know what the word Fakir means
And they will confuse me with those darned fruit machines
And a man who was tight showed unseemly delight
When his card was delivered just here
He got all worked up when his friend tried to speak
And said 'Don't stop me now on a good winning streak'
And changed two pounds for pennies and left me quite weak
For I'm the only Fakir on the Pier.

[165]

There is one thing that remains indelible in my memory. As Queen Mary left the theatre she spoke to the standing audience and said 'Wasn't it good'.

For the opening scene, there was no curtain and as the audience assembled, the empty stage was dimly lit. Lying invisible across the stage was a long, very thin wood batten. Attached to each end was the thinnest of wires. On cue, the company assembled in a leisurely manner and the moment the curtain-music started they formed a straight line. Up went the lights, up went the batten of wood and the audience was confronted with a line of ghastly stage smiles which raised the first laugh. Then straight into the opening chorus with music by Jack Strachey and words by Michael Treford.

ACKNOWLEDGEMENTS

We wish to thank Kayser-Bondor for the lights
We wish to thank Strand Electric for the tights
Abdullah's did the furniture we're using in the show
The cigarettes supplied by Old Times Furnishing & Co
We wish to thank Cecil Beaton for the wigs
Yes – and Gustave for the sets and curtains too
And for the generous applause for all our pre-arranged encores
We particularly want to thank you.

We feel our material should get some panegyrics
Moss Brothers did the music – Morris Angel wrote the lyrics
Drinks by Sanitas – smoke by Insulin
And the theatre's disinfected throughout – with gin
The lovely ladies dresses are by Horne's of Upper Tooting
Darling Norman Hartnell did the nicely natty suiting
Production by a miracle – with errors and omissions
Musicians by arrangement – and arrangements by musicians.

We wish to thank for our contracts – Mr Wyse
To get this job was a wonderful surprise
The exits and the entrances – by force of circumstance
Productions and all stage effects by accident or chance
We wish to thank some attractive little Muse
Who deals with inspiration for revues
And for the flowers at the end – which we have paid someone to send
We particularly want to Thank You!

[166]

Cast of *The Bolton's Revue* on stage.

There was talk of a move into the West End. John Wyse had agreed if we transferred that nobody would be replaced and everyone would receive proper 'West End' salaries. It was a choice between the only two vacant theatres, The Playhouse and St James. Neither was really suitable, but J. P. Mitchell, who took over the financial reins, chose the latter. In a modest way *Bolton's Revue* helped to make stage history. It was the first revue ever staged in the long and venerable life of the St James Theatre. I am sure the ghosts of Sir George Alexander, Pinero and Oscar Wilde would have found much to enjoy in our entertainment.

Out of the acorns in our show, big trees grew. Patricia Dainton became a film star in *The Dancing Years*, Richard Gilbert a successful T.V. Director, Sheila Matthews was later successful on stage and television and Daphne Anderson is doing very well in both these mediums. At the moment of writing, Daphne is playing for film star Jean Simmons in *A Little Night Music* at the Adelphi Theatre. In the same show she also renders a similar service in the case of indisposition for Hermione Gingold.

A nightmare that returns from time to time was the sight and sound of four strong men wrestling to get my baby grand piano up the iron staircase leading to the stage-door of the Torch Theatre (commonly known as the Torture Theatre) in Knightsbridge, only to find it was locked. I bought this valuable piano (valuable in memories) from Mrs Gladys Henson, wife of Leslie Henson, for sentimental reasons. So many 'greats' had played on it at the Henson's Saturday night parties at their home in St John's Wood: Noël Coward, Cole Porter, Ivor Novello and Vivian Ellis. Now just because this little theatre hadn't a piano, it was being subjected to this monstrous treatment.

The whole episode stemmed from the fact that I saw a photo in a window of a girl I'd seen who was excellent in intimate revue, Charmian Innes. Although I hadn't previously met her, I telephoned and suggested we should do a *Revue for Two*. She agreed. We both had enough personal material for two solo spots to fill Act One. For Act Two we demonstrated the difference between Music Hall and Cabaret and closed with six singles and a duet, with Bob Martin at the piano. The press liked us. It led to more work and our meeting two years later, in revue. Peter Reynolds, the actor, and his brother ran the theatre at that time. Both were a little vague to put it mildly. For example, we sat up nights addressing and stamping envelopes containing the announcement of our *Revue for Two*, and when I found there was no response from my personal friends, I discovered they had forgotten to post the 500 envelopes!

[168]

The 'No Orchids for my Lady' number with Donald Reed and chorus.

A number from *Billy Milton's Party*: Johnny Ladd, Clive Dunn and chorus.

CHAPTER FIFTEEN

The Windmill and Other Odds and Sods

I WAS ASKED TO PRODUCE ANOTHER REVUE FOR THE BOLTON'S Theatre Club, called *Billy Milton's Party*. The cabaret star Daphne Barker, a youthful Clive Dunn (later star in 'Dad's Army'), young Lionel Blair (now producer), ex-opera star Rose Hill and T.V.'s Daphne Oxenford were in the cast. For our Sunday shows we had guest artists such as Fenella Fielding, Yvonne Mitchell and Adelaide Hall.

After the final performance I went to Brighton for a weekend. Walking along the front I met the owner of Hurseal Radiators of Regent Street. He made me an offer, as a side line, to join him and the Marquess of Milford Haven in the promotion of his hermetically-sealed and thermostatically-controlled radiators. When I called on Vivian Van Damm, who directed London's Windmill Theatre, he gave me an order straight away. As I was leaving his office 'V.D.' said to me 'You can have a season here, Billy. Forty pounds a week, five shows a day, start in a fortnight.' I said 'Thanks V.D.' and that concluded my short excursion into the business world.

To protect his lovelies, V.D. made the men dress at the top of the building and the girls in the basement. Who, after climbing up and down fifty stairs, five times a day, would have the energy to attack anyone? The midday audience were responsive, but after that the patrons stayed on, changing seats at the end of each show, gradually working their way to the front to get a better view of the girls. The orchestra's drummer was perched on a rostrum, which enabled him not only to watch the stage, but also to keep an eye on anything unusual taking place under gentlemen's hats or newspapers.

Peter Sellers, Alfred Marks, Kenneth More, Jimmy Edwards and Harry Worth, all started at the Windmill. It was a tough place to work but you had to remember the audience had come to see the nudes, not you.

The torture of our profession lies in the possibility that your endurance, health and money may give out before you achieve your quota of success. On reflection, it is amazing how much the brain and body will stand because, as well as five shows a day, I rehearsed a new cabaret act with Daphne Barker during the intervals and did a sixth show at 1.00 a.m. at the Bagatelle Restaurant, accompanied by Edmundo Ros and His Orchestra. Incidentally, the manager of the Bagatelle was Harry Levene (later famous international boxing promoter).

We managed to slip in a Charity Ball at the Dorchester Hotel, when the guest of honour was Prince Philip. As Daphne curtsied and I shook his hand, he said *sotto voce* 'What are you two doing here?' He didn't realise we were the Cabaret. For inclusion in our night-club act, we had been rehearsing a risqué number called 'The Family Bed', which was hardly a song for a charity function. I was flabbergasted when I heard Daphne announce it as our next number. But she was right in her judgement; it made the po-faced straitlaced charity audience sit up, particularly as the laughter and applause was led by Prince Philip.

Back at the Bagatelle, just before we were due to go on, there was a knock on the dressing-room door; it was a young man. 'Can I speak to Miss Barker?' I gave Daphne a shout and when she appeared he enquired 'Miss Barker?' When she replied 'Yes', he slapped a writ in her hand. Instead of being annoyed, as I thought she would be, she became tearful. It appeared she had given a boy-friend cash to settle outstanding bills and he had spent the money on himself. I consoled her as best I could and said 'Darling, if you want to cry, we'll go on later'. She rounded on me angrily and said 'Certainly not! We'll do the act now – I'll cry later!'

Army stories were popular in those days. One in the act always went well – it was about a new recruit.

'What's your name?' yelled the sergeant.

'Kettle' replied the recruit.

'How do you spell it?'

'K-e-t-t-l-e.'

'Are you married?'

Daphne Barker and I in cabaret.

'Yes.'

'What's your wife's name?'

'Lydova.'

'How do you spell it?'

'L-y-d-o-v-a Kettle, sarge.'

'Any kids?'

'Yes, three. Two with spouts and one without.'

Playing West End Night Clubs brought me into contact with so many people. I often had difficulty in placing them. I was crossing Leicester Square one day and felt I knew the smartly-dressed man coming towards me. He looked like an actor and as I didn't want to cut him, I said 'Hello, how's the show going?' I couldn't for the life of me think of what show, but thought this opening gambit might give me a clue. He replied 'Fine'. Still groping, I asked 'How long have you been running?' 'Quite a few years now', he commented. 'Oh', I ventured, 'You're in *The Mousetrap*?' 'No, I'm in the gentlemen's toilet at Quaglino's.' Then the penny dropped. It was he, when I played cabaret at Quag's, who had kept me up-to-date nightly with new stories the patrons told him while washing their hands.

At Quag's I had an ardent fan, a society woman who followed me wherever I appeared. Years ago she had appealed to men – but none of them ever listened. Unfortunately, whenever she was intoxicated, she became a kleptomaniac and the silver cutlery would start disappearing into her voluminous handbag. The Maître d'Hotel knew her weakness and as she was a good customer, found the only way to retrieve the property was to ask her to sing. She had a lovely voice and was always willing to oblige. As she stood by the piano, she was quite unconscious of the fact that a waiter was surreptitiously removing the knives and forks from her handbag. The amusing part was the look of astonishment on her face when she picked up her bag again and found it much lighter than expected.

Lady Broadhurst invited me to entertain at her husband's birthday party at their house in Grosvenor Square. When I arrived, I found they were still at dinner. I noticed the piano had been moved to the spacious entrance hall, where I was to perform, and put too near the big log-fire which was blazing fiercely. The woodwork had started to blister and the heat had sent it out of tune. That was bad enough, but when I saw the walls were covered with antique clocks, ticking away merrily – I feared the worst. It was just 10.00 p.m. as I was singing enthusiastically 'I'll climb the highest Mountain' and the whole bloody lot started to chime!

Daphne Barker and I at the Theatrical Garden Party at Richmond in one of our numbers from the Bagatelle.

The Paradise Club in Regent Street attracted a mixed-bag of customers. Prior to working there myself, I went to the opening night of Inga Anderson, the Danish-Canadian songstress. She had apparently antagonised the band, because for her entrance music they played 'The Dead March' and the man on the spotlight put a green lime on her gold-lamé gown. Later, as Inga was having supper with me after her show, a male customer whom she had reproved sharply for his noisy behaviour during her act, stubbed out his cigar on her Sole Bonne Femme.

I had similar incidents, not every night passed peacefully. At one performance I had a heckler I didn't know how to get rid of. He blew me a raspberry. I stopped, took the microphone over to his table and said, 'Sir, that was the best raspberry I have ever heard. Would you give us an encore?' He did and, to my delight, the customers complained. He was removed.

I always start my act by singing a verse which gives me an idea of what sort of an audience I am entertaining. It goes like this . . .

'Earning my living is a bit beneath my station,
But I run a little bureau of exclusive information.
My service is unique and quite the best thing of its class
And I find time passes quickly, as I sit here on my stool and
    let it pass.'

If they laugh I know I'm okay, but on this occasion there was no laugh, because unbeknown to me, a man behind my back had appeared, bringing me a glass of champagne. This he repeated at intervals during the whole of my thirty-minute act. Thank heaven the audience good-naturedly greeted his every appearance with applause.

I rarely got to bed before dawn and would often breakfast at the old Lyons Corner House in Coventry Street, Piccadilly, which was open all night and was a rendezvous for artists, musicians, pimps, ponces, prostitutes and homosexuals. I remember the night one woman in particular caught my attention. She was pleasantly plump, middle-aged and wore a frilly blouse, two rows of pearls, blue coat, skirt and long gloves. She ate too daintily for words. Whenever she picked up a piece of toast there was such a palaver before it actually reached her tiny rosebud mouth, it fascinated me. I asked my waiter about her. He laughed and said 'He's a harmless old queen who comes here quite often. Have a look at her legs – they're like tree trunks!'

To end on a grander note, I was honoured to be chosen as the act most suitable for the Gala Performance at the Mayfair Hotel to welcome their Majesties King George and Queen Elizabeth, back from their tour of Canada and the U.S.A. It was an enjoyable contrast. Working at the Windmill led to a spate of music hall dates, working on bills with Dorothy Squires, Evelyn Laye and Ethel Revnell. It sharpened and broadened my act and I found that artists on the halls were warm-hearted. There was more bonhomie on that side of the profession than on any other.

CHAPTER SIXTEEN

Polypurgatory

TWO SOUTH AFRICANS OFFERED TO FINANCE A THIRD REVUE AT the Bolton's Theatre. I had been warned they were difficult to handle, but as I had just finished producing a show for Daniel Mayer Ltd., I felt I could manage them. How wrong I was. They wanted a show that would outfringe the fringe, but I knew the audience at Bolton's preferred to hear the gentle click of the croquet balls. We argued and wrangled and finally I bowed out. I was sick at heart with the whole business. I felt I had to get away from everything to do with theatre. So I went to the Labour Exchange!

The interviewer appeared to be very much the son of a gentleman, but turned out to be a son of a bitch. In a superior manner he enquired 'I suppose you speak languages?' 'I do' I snorted. This exchange led to a further interview, this time with a butch lady who had a small moustache and a baritone voice. 'You look rather mature for what we want' she boomed. 'A Polytechnic Guide at the Grand Mattenhof Hotel, Interlaken, Switzerland. The salary is £6 a week, all found, plus return fare.' I nodded my acceptance – anything to get out of England. I soon found this new life was equally honeycombed with the same thing I was running away from.

For a start, dreading heights as I do, one of my first duties was to take the tourists up the Jungfrau, 13,993 feet! I recall arriving at the summit,

CLAP YOUR HANDS
(THERE'S A GOOD TIME COMING)
by
HARRY S. PEPPER &
BILLY MILTON.
As
Sung & Danced
in ARCHIE PITT's
Super Musical Production
"The Show's The Thing"
Featuring GRACIE FIELDS
BURFORD PUBLISHING Co.
SELLING AGENTS
DIX LTD.,
7, DENMARK ST., W.C.2.
2/- NET

F.J.H
A SONG FOX-TROT
Wand'ring Around
Written & Composed by
BILLY MILTON &
HARRY S. PEPPER
Featured by
BILLY MILTON
IN LADDIE CLIFF'S SUCCESSFUL PRODUCTION THE
BOW-WOWS
at the
PRINCE OF WALES THEATRE.
LONDON, W.C.2.
DIX LTD.
INTERNATIONAL MUSIC PUBLISHERS
7, DENMARK STREET. CHARING CROSS ROAD.
2/-

breathless and blue with cold, but consoling myself with the thought I wouldn't run into any theatricals, only to hear Jack Hylton say 'What the hell are you doing here, Billy?'

It was my duty to take the guests once a week to the Casino, where they would avidly watch the Swiss entertainers slap their bottoms and toss the flags – lovely the first time, but monotonous on repetition. When I had my night off, I would creep back into the hotel very late and avoid ringing the night-porter's noisy bell by knocking gently; and he'd let me in. The manager didn't like me. He was always puzzled to know which of his staff was the late-comer. I lived on the third floor, so to fool him I took the lift to the fourth and before he had time to put on his dressing gown and open his door, I had run to the third and was safely in my room.

On Thursday nights the guests danced to a radiogram. I didn't look forward to that as I had to partner the wallflowers – ladies of sundry shapes and sizes. The only good thing to come out of it was I lost pounds in weight doing so. There was a change of scene on Sunday mornings. I gave out the hymn books and played the piano; hymns of course.

One of our new arrivals was a smart-looking woman who had unfortunately been over-booked. This caused the manager and his wife to vacate their first-floor apartment (with balcony) for the guest, until she could be re-accommodated. As a friendly gesture I suggested we might take a short ramble in the woods, but she had already noticed that military manoeuvres were taking place in an adjacent field. She said she preferred to watch them. After a few days her proper reservation became available and the manager and his wife moved back into their own apartment. Around 6.00 that evening I heard a scream and dashed downstairs to find the manager's wife with her dress half-over her head, and a young soldier's backside rapidly disappearing over the balcony. He was obviously one of the militia who had enjoyed the lady-guest's own manoeuvres, but was unaware of the transfer.

I had a terrifying experience when a substantial earth-tremor plus a small tornado swept across Lake Brienze. It removed the roof clean off the big chalet at the end of our garden, uprooted trees like weeds and finally disappeared over the mountain. Generally speaking, the season was enjoyable and the head of the Polytechnic, Commander Studd, suggested I work the following year at Tremezzo in Northern Italy.

Henry and Alice Sides managed the peaceful old-fashioned lake-side hotel at Tremezzo and we were to become lifelong friends. I felt this would be a good season and the superb weather egged everyone to amorous exploits. After lunch, I would see the English girls climbing on the pillion-seats of the handsome Italian waiters, only too impatient to get away from mother, and looking forward to being whisked away to the countryside for passionate pastoral pleasures.

Twice a week I visited Venice with coach-loads of tourists, leaving the hotel at 6.00 a.m., lunch at Lake Garda, a pause at Verona and arrive in Venice at 2.00 p.m. On the return journey, I lolled back in my comfortable solo-seat reserved for the guide, occasionally chattering into the microphone with informative and amusing comments about the countryside, buildings and people. I thought to myself 'In the past, I have lived every day as though it was my last. I must change my ways and try to save instead of spend.' I would need a new wardrobe when I returned to England, so I decided to utilize some of the guides' tricks. I announced to those travelling in the thirty-eight seater that Anna, the coach-driver's wife, was shortly to present him with a baby – applause from the sympathetic mums. If they felt they would like to donate a 'little something' to lighten their financial load, I was sure it would be greatly appreciated, but of course it was entirely up to them. The collection was substantial. What they did not know was the Italian driver was a bachelor and did not understand a word I said.

St Moritz was on my tour list and the cartons of cigarettes I purchased there found their way into the hands of the ticket collector at the arena in Verona. The U.S. Navy in Venice supplied my wholesaler with as many cartons of Lucky Strike and Chesterfield cigarettes as I needed to take back to the hall-porter at our hotel in Tremezzo. I also had an arrangement with the major-domo who stood in front of St Mark's Church. He denied entrance to any ladies without head-covering and rented out scarves (of which he had dozens). Even the man in charge of the Golden Altar would tell me how many tickets I needed to pay for. Everyone was on the merry summer-fiddle.

Our guides were forbidden to take guests to the glass factories, as it was common knowledge they received substantial commissions. A way had to be devised to get round this. On entering the Piazza San Marco, most tourists want to take photographs. I advised them the best place to take photos was from the left-hand side of the square, because I had previously arranged to meet casually a glass-factory representative there. It worked perfectly. First he would recognise me and say 'Hello, Mr Milton'. I would pretend surprise and suggest to my tourists that perhaps they might like to follow my friend who owned the glass factory, as I was not allowed

PAQUITA
A Tango Song
WORDS & MUSIC BY
BILLY MILTON & BASIL BARTLETT
Sung by
Billy Milton
IN THE WARNER BROS. FILM
"THE CALL of the SEA"
PHOTO BY
CYRIL STANBOROUGH
DIX LTD.,
24, DENMARK ST.,
LONDON
W.C.2
6D
COPYRIGHT.

to take them to see how the beautiful glass ornaments were made. I would then make my way to a nearby café, order a bottle of Orvieto and watch the pigeons in the square, while *my* pigeons were helping to contribute to my new suits with a twenty-five per cent commission on everything they bought.

One day I was in charge of two gondolas slowly making their way down the Grand Canal. I was thoroughly enjoying every moment of my well-informed discourse on the magnificent palaces we were passing when an elderly lady in the other boat complained she couldn't hear what I was saying. Gallantly I indicated to draw the gondolas together so that I could step into the other boat. As I was about to do so, the wake of a passing motor-boat prised the boats apart and I fell gracefully into the canal. I wouldn't have minded the tourists' laughter if it hadn't been for the fact that a good suit was ruined.

After dinner I took the usual excursion on the lagoon. As the moonlight danced like diamonds on the dense, dark water, I started to daydream as the water lapped gently against the sides of the gondola. I was brought back to reality when a loud voice made the most shattering remark of all time. 'What Venice needs is a bloody good wash with soap and water!' If I'd had a hatchet handy I would have happily buried it in that thick, insensitive skull.

The real comedy came when I had to gather my flock for the journey home. Everyone was assembled in the coach except for three elderly men, when it started to rain, heavily. Then one made his way tipsily to the coach, but the other two were missing. I went to look for them in nearby bars, while the rest of the passengers grumbled about being kept waiting. Dripping wet, I found the missing men and guided them back only to find that their friend had left the coach again to search for his mates. Thank heaven I had the next day off.

Back in Tremezzo I unwound in a lakeside café with a large flask of Chianti. Slowly I got into the mood to do my realistic impression of a dog barking, at which I excel when pickled. About midnight I launched my first bark across the lake towards Bellargio, just opposite Tremezzo. My voice carried quite clearly across to the other side. Dogs there started to bark. A few minutes later the dogs on my side answered and so the cacophony went on until I tottered to bed, contented. Crazy, I know, but I thought it was fun.

As I was dining with an Italian friend on the terrace of the smart Martinez Restaurant in Venice, our quiet conversation was interrupted by the

I'VE GOT A MAN

WRITTEN BY

CLIFFORD SEYLER

COMPOSED BY

BILLY MILTON

SUNG BY

GRACIE FIELDS.

B.3203. H.M.V Record

London: **FRANCIS, DAY & HUNTER LTD.**
138-140, CHARING CROSS ROAD W.C 2

NEW YORK AGENTS: LEO FEIST, Inc., 231-5, WEST 40TH STREET.
SYDNEY AGENTS: J.ALBERT & SON, 137-139, KING STREET.
PARIS AGENTS: PUBLICATIONS, FRANCIS-DAY S.A., 30, RUE DE L'ECHIQUIER.
BERLIN AGENTS: FRANCIS, DAY & HUNTER G.mb.H. LEIPZIGER STR 37. W.8.

6^D
NET.

PRINTED IN ENGLAND.

She's a Good, Good Girl!
FOX TROT
FEATURED & RECORDED BY
PHOTO BY HOWARD AND JOAN COSTER.
Ross and Sargent.
WORDS AND MUSIC BY
BILLY MILTON
COPYRIGHT IN ALL COUNTRIES.
ALL RIGHTS RESERVED
6d
PRINTED IN SCOTLAND
PETER MAURICE & CO LTD
36-38 WIGMORE STREET, LONDON, W.L.

strident tones of an American woman placing her guests. It was a sharp
contrast to the voice of an English tourist who had just complained 'I can't
eat this Italian muck, bring me some good old Roast Beef and Yorkshire'.
As my back was towards the American lady of the grating voice, I
turned. It was the Duchess of Windsor.

Her party consisted of the Duke, Oliver Messel (whom I knew well),
and three young men. Oliver told me he was in Venice to do the interior
decoration of Barbara Hutton's Palazzo.

The Duchess took the top of the table. She was beautifully dressed in a
rigid sort of way. Her hair was so meticulously arranged she could have
posed as a wax model in any shop window. She proceeded to dominate
the conversation with her candid and caustic comments. I became un-
pleasantly aware of her tremendous drive, assurance and possessiveness.
The Duke said very little and seemed to never take his eyes off her. It was
an eerie experience for me to be within feet of the woman who caused a
king to forget his duty.

The reaction of some English acquaintances on holiday who had seen
me on stage and T.V., brought home to me the fact they thought I was
down on my luck. Although I had thoroughly enjoyed myself, I realised I
musn't continue this way if I was to carry on in my real profession. Fate
then took a hand when, during a violent thunderstorm, I received a call
from Richard Gilbert, B.B.C. television director in London. 'Would you
like to do a monthly T.V. series for us entitled "As Time Goes By" – songs
at the piano plus a celebrity guest?' I had a feeling it might be a practical
joke. I shouted 'Sorry, can't hear you because of the storm. Send me a
wire.' And it was for real! Poly kindly released me for the rest of the season.
I flew back home. I was in show business again.

CHAPTER SEVENTEEN

Pantomime

AGNES LITTLER WAS A DEVOTED MOTHER OF THREE CHILDREN: Prince, Emile and Blanche. Towards the end of her life she was deeply concerned that her two sons were not on speaking terms with each other. Just before she died she begged them to be friends again, but they were irreconcilable.

Blanche devoted every day to her mother and it was through my long friendship, both socially and professionally, with Blanche, that I came to meet Agnes. I grew fond of her, tried to cheer her up and take her mind off the inevitable. Each week I sent her a postcard of cats, dogs or flowers – it developed into a ritual. Through the years it built up into quite a collection and I'm told they have been preserved in albums and given to the Littler children.

My friendship with Blanche (now Lady Robey O.B.E.) started in 1948, when she first saw me in *Bolton's Revue* dressed as an Edwardian lady of 1908, straight from the chorus of Daly's Theatre, singing . . .

> 'Oh, I'm known in every Hotel
> As a cracked Edwardian Belle'

Blanche decided there and then I was to be her 'Dame' Sarah in *Dick Whittington*, the pantomime she was to present at the King's Theatre, Hammersmith. The cast included Liz Webb as Principal Boy, the *Bumper*

Sir George Robey in *Touch Wood and Whistle*.

Fun Book comedian Robert Moreton and Grace Mars, a singer discovery of Richard Afton, the *Evening News* correspondent.

During rehearsals, I was sitting with Blanche in the stalls when she was approached by Grace Mars' mother. Mrs Mars felt the costumes for her daughter did not compare in splendour with those of Liz Webb. She asked Blanche 'May I have your permission to have my daughter's dresses made privately at my expense?' Blanche had a presentiment this was going to happen and gave me a quick, mischievous glance (as if to say 'That will save us some money'), before she replied 'Certainly, Mrs Mars, if it would make you happy'.

Playing Dame can be a gamble, you can't fool children. They either like you or they don't. I was lucky, they liked me. Perhaps it was because I love children and family audiences; the toddlers sucking their thumbs and big fat kids scratching their tums.

Dick Whittington's Cat was a great favourite. The youngsters loved the scene where Pussy whispered in my ear all the naughty things he'd been up to the previous night. My facial expressions of surprise and disbelief brought squeals of delight. For punishment I gave him a bath – which he hated. Then I dried and powdered him with a huge puff. First his face, then chest, and finally lifting his tail, to powder his bottom. One thing I did learn and had never realised before, was the disappointment of many young children, when Pussy, taking his bow in the finale, removed his head. It shattered their illusions.

Backstage life was fairly normal apart from an odd episode. One of the ladies was having an affair with the muscular deep-sea-diver who appeared in the under-water ballet sequence. It was so energy-sapping that it began to affect his performance and one night he bungled the feature trick in which his partner dived from a height into his arms below, and nearly dropped her. Later in their dressing room which was next to mine, the dainty fish-girl became an angry fish-wife and I couldn't help hearing the noise of various objects being thrown about.

Pantomime was certainly an experience and to commemorate our first contact with it, Michael Treford and I wrote a Panto song which was later used in revue.

FAIRY BLUE BELL

I'm a Fairy Blue Bell
Tho' at heart an honest girl

Tommy Fields, members of the cast, Olive Lucious and I in *No, No, Nanette*.

I have contours that compel
When I played Dick Whittington last year
I had my name in lights – all over Wigan Pier.

The Demon King pursued me through the Dell
But I still had my tights on when I fell
He just adored my profile and idolised my hips
And said 'Come out to supper' as he kissed me on the lips
But I told him with great dignity
Where to put his fish and chips.

An oversexed young Daffodil who simply loved a lark
Kept flirting with the Fairies who came dancing through the dark
But now he's been transplanted to a Hot-Bed in Hyde Park
And left little Fairy Blue Bell.

I thought a young Narcissus with his face as white as chalk
Was wriggling with passion till he said in Fairies' talk
It's not love – it's a Caterpillar climbing up my stalk
Poor thwarted Fairy Blue Bell.

When the curtain fell on the last performance of *Dick Whittington*,
Blanche invited me to appear in a revue called *Touch Wood and Whistle*,
that she was mounting for her husband, Sir George Robey.

Before rehearsals were due to start, I went for a holiday to Tangier. On
the plane I got into conversation with a young fellow sitting next to me.
We talked until the plane landed at Gibraltar, where we were supposed to
transfer to another plane to take us on to Tangier. Due to engine trouble,
the flight was delayed and we had to stay overnight at the Rock Hotel.
We dined together and later had a drink at the bar. He enquired as to what
I did for a living. I played it low and said I was an actor, but ready to take
any work, if it was legal. Next morning he suggested we travel to Tangier
by boat instead of plane – slower, but more picturesque. I agreed and
during our conversation he indicated that plenty of money could be made
out of a little light smuggling. The cargo was nothing more deadly than
cigarettes and the trip to Algeciras in Spain was short. It was 'money for
old coconuts', he said. He suggested I think about it and meet him a few
days hence at the Riff Hotel in Tangier.

I had a friend in Tangier and told him of the proposal. He advised
strongly against it and said 'It used to be easy, but recently smuggling has
become a dangerous occupation'.

I appeared in several 'Early to Braden' shows; this was a sketch called
'Most Happy Killer'.
[BBC COPYRIGHT PHOTOGRAPH]

Frankly, I'd toyed with the idea, thinking it might be fun, but on his advice I didn't keep the appointment. I was lucky. I later learned a young American who did the trip in a boat, was pounced upon by an armed customs-vessel and the crew and cargo impounded. Prison sentence followed. Jail in that part of the world, with the hot climate and shocking conditions, wouldn't have been fun.

Blanche Littler's *Touch Wood and Whistle* provided me with the opportunity to gain more experience in music hall and a chance to work with Sir George Robey who was indeed 'The Prime Minister of Mirth'. Apart from my solo act I partnered Charmian Innes, with whom I had worked previously in *Revue for Two*: a talented young lady, but not easy to work with.

After a few weeks Charmian said she was not happy with her billing, material and salary. Blanche wrote her a note saying she would like to make her happy, so from next Saturday she had better look for happiness elsewhere. Charmian was shaking from top to toe when I held her hand in the finale that night. I thought she had fever, but she was shaking with anger. I did not know about the note.

Jack Payne, the bandleader, was my agent at the time and I got in touch with him when an Australian friend asked me to try and find a job for a young lady friend of his. She was good at figures and Jack employed her in his contract department. She was a beautiful girl and Jack fell for her. Some time later, a visit to Paris had to be arranged so that she could get medical attention for a 'forthcoming event' which was to be terminated. Jack seemed remarkably unconcerned about her welfare. This hurt and enraged the girl and after her convalescence she returned to London, determined on revenge.

Frankie Howerd, the up-and-coming comedian, was one of Payne's star clients. An anonymous letter reached Frankie at the London Palladium where he was appearing, which asked whether he was aware he was earning a great deal more than he was being paid by his agent. That put the cat among the pigeons and the result was a lengthy and much publicised court case which was won by Frankie Howerd.

My life is governed by the telephone; it can be a devil or an angel. Once, while I was playing with my worry-beads, it rang. 'Are you free?' asked the voice of producer Stanley Willis Croft who was one of the kindest men in the business. 'Yes!' He replied 'Good. You open Monday fortnight, co-starring with Tommy Fields [Gracie's tall, toothy and talented brother] at the Empire, Liverpool, in *No, No, Nanette*.'

[194]

The final scene of *Lilac Time*, I am fifth from the left, playing Mr Veidt.

I asked myself – at the age of fifty-five, could I learn the long script and all the dances in time? I certainly could! Would it be a success? It certainly would, and it was! With the wonderful 'Tea for Two' and 'I want to be Happy' score, how could it fail?

Tommy and I were old friends and team work in this show is the most important thing. My duet with Olive Lucious who played my wife, 'You can dance with any Girl', brought the house down when, during the dance, she grabbed me by the scruff of the neck and seat of my pants and marched me off stage. I also enjoyed the fun in the number 'Take a little One-Step' when six gentlemen of the chorus raised my bulky frame above their heads, paused for a moment, while I remarked with pained emphasis 'Gentlemen, you really *must* cut your nails!'

When the show came to an end and the sound of the 'Goodbyes' was fading away, I'd hardly had time to re-adjust my travelling rug when the phone rang again. I happened to be lying on my water-bed when that angel of good news, Stanley Willis Croft said 'Billy, I want you to play Mr Veidt in *Lilac Time*'. That simple opening-line led me to the second longest engagement of my theatrical career.

For three years (on and off), I was to play the jolly father of three daughters in the lovely musical based on Schubert's music and adapted by Heinrich Berté. John Hanson's magnificent voice and consistent performances played a major part in the success of the show. Then when we thought it was all over, an offer came to play South Africa. Due to other commitments John could not accept and his role was taken by Thomas Round, star of the D'Oyly Carte Opera Company, and petite Marian Studholme played Lili.

We opened at Her Majesty's Theatre in Johannesburg, a beautiful theatre with seats for 2,000 and excellent backstage conditions. Dressing-room facilities were first-class: bathroom, toilet and lounge to receive guests; the things architects often forget to include, and the sort of things that make an artist happy which reflects in their performance. Johannesburg is 3,500 feet above sea-level and any vigorous on-stage action leaves you breathless. Oxygen-cylinders (with masks attached) were placed at each side of the stage for artists to use. It was while I was having a sniff one night after my waltz number with Mrs Veidt, I decided to make a change of direction in my future life.

I thought 'No more touring'. It had been fun. First it was 'Get me Billy Milton', then 'Get me a type like Billy Milton' and before they could say 'Who is Billy Milton?', a change must be made. It was time for the piano.

CHAPTER EIGHTEEN

Second String to my Bow

ENTERING AT THE PIANO IN PRESTIGE HOTELS IS LUCRATIVE and consistent. In my case it enables me to live at home in my studio in Holland Street, Kensington, and to accept television and radio work. The development of this asset happened in this way.

Joan Davis, producer and dance director of many London Palladium shows, invited my agent Michael Summerton and myself to holiday at her villa in Menton. Towards the end of the holiday Joan motored us to Eze where we dined at a restaurant overlooking the moonlit Mediterranean. We then journeyed on to attend one of the last concerts Sir John Barbirolli gave in the courtyard of Prince and Princess Rainier's palace in Monte Carlo. Michael enjoyed the concert, but was insistent we spend our last days in Cannes. We lunched on the Carlton Hotel beach. Michael bathed while I slept on a Lilo. As I lay dreaming, somebody shook me. It was Dennis Fine who supplies Danny La Rue with the marvellously extravagant furs for his shows. His first words were my favourite off-putters. 'What are you doing here?' Sleepily I replied 'I'm going home tomorrow'. He said 'I'll give you a ring'.

Back in London he introduced me to Danny La Rue at his club, which was then in Hanover Square, W.1. A friend of Danny's, the property dealer David G. Lowes, had bought The United Hunts Club off Park Lane and wanted an entertainer at the piano. The following day Danny's Rolls

picked me up and took me to the club to audition. The engagement lasted
four and a half years. Fate moves in a strange way; it was Michael's insistence that we spent the last day of our holiday in Cannes that started this
chain of events.

The United Hunts Club had a membership which read like Debrett. To
mention but a few: Lord Mountbatten, the Dame of Sark, the Marquess of
Milford Haven and Lady Cadogan – and there were a few eccentrics as
well. Colonel Walter Fitzgibbon-Walter was a frequent visitor. Directly
he arrived I would hear him say to the head-waiter 'Tell the bloody pianist
to play "Some Enchanted Evening"'. A glass of champagne would then
arrive. If I switched to anything else, he snorted 'What the hell do you
think you're doing? Back to my tune!' Along would come another glass
of champers. The furious looks of the other members could have killed
the colonel but his hide was as thick as a rhinoceros's. He was worth a lot of
Lanson black-label to the club!

There was also a tweedy-type lady from Maidenhead who bred Corgis.
When in her cups she would proceed to lie under the piano, surrounded
by her dogs and 'listen' to my music. Another member, Lady C., had a
ruthless gracefulness about her. When in a playful mood, she had the
painful habit of stamping on your foot with the heel of her shoe. Thank
heavens I escaped as I was protected by the piano.

During this engagement the Boulting Brothers offered me the role of
the Archbishop's chaplain in the Peter Sellers film *Heavens Above*. I got
one of the first laughs in the picture when I answered the telephone and
listened intently to a vicar. On replacing the receiver, I remarked wistfully
'Sometimes I wish the Boy Scout movement had never been thought of!'
Peter and I were filming a scene in the quadrangle of Keble College,
Oxford. I thought it would be nice to have a picture of Peter and myself
for my gallery of stars. When the day's work had been successfully put in
the 'can', I walked towards him as he sat in his chair. Before I could reach
him the first assistant intervened. He questioned my motives and I was
told to wait while he passed on my request to Sellers. After a pause he
nodded, then another chair was brought. I sat. Not a word was spoken.
Click, click, click went the still-photographer's camera. I was then quickly
ushered away. Needless to say, I never received the photographs.

I cannot help contrasting this incident with another – when I worked
with George Raft. There was no chi-chi to my request. It was 'Sure,
okay!' and the photograph is one of my treasured possessions. I was
playing a cameo-part in his first English film, which was made at Walton-

I played a small role in George Raft's first English film – *Two Guys Abroad*.

on-Thames. I liked the way he insisted that all the barmen in the club scene were to be ex-boxing champions: Ted 'Kid' Lewis, Freddie Mills and Dave Crowley. Supporting him in the picture was the American boxing champion, Maxie Rosenbloom. Though Raft was well into his sixties, when it came to his 'snake-hips dance' he was still the tops. Why the picture was never released in this country I shall never know.

When I was in Hollywood, Raft was under contract to Paramount. He was at the top of his career. One day, having breakfast in my bungalow at the Garden of Allah, I read the headlines in the *Los Angeles Times* – 'Raft to give evidence at Bugsy Siegal's trial'. A bomb had been tossed into another gangster's home. Raft stood to lose a lot if he went through with it, but that's what he did and consequently suffered a considerable loss of popularity. When in later years he accepted the position of host at the Colony Club, Berkeley Square, Mayfair, he was refused permission to return to this country after a trip to the States, because of his alleged connections with the Mafia.

Heavens Above led me to *Hot Millions* with Peter Ustinov, filmed for M.G.M. at their Elstree Studios. Peter and I first met at a charity matinée at His Majesty's Theatre. After the show he dropped me off at my studio and came in for a drink. I think the best acting I've ever seen was on the day that Peter presented his bill for re-writing the script to the wealthy lady who was financing *Hot Millions*. She wasn't famed for her generosity and her reaction from her customary bright executive-smile to slow shock was superb! My role was that of a Frenchman who didn't speak a word of English. I was the owner of a café and Peter wanted to rent the top floor. It was nothing more than an artist's studio with large nudes painted on the walls. Laughs came from the fact that everything I said or did, Peter mis-interpreted and vice-versa.

Speaking French brought me several interviews with casting directors. I recall two with dubious pleasure. First was a powerful casting-directress, a denizen of the deep and sometimes dubious world of the cinema. I had been warned to be wary of her as she had so many chips on her shoulder – all she needed was some fish to go with them. While I was recovering from the sight of her and from the draught created by her false eyelashes that were operating like agitated butterfly wings, I became aware that a steely voice had asked me 'Can you speak French?' Covering my con-fusion I hastily replied 'Fluently'.

My fluent French didn't endear me to an American director, a tall, grey-headed burnt-out satyr. Sitting in his office at Elstree Studios, he

I played a Frenchman in *Hot Millions*, this starred Peter Ustinov.

informed me in a somewhat challenging voice, that he had lived in Paris. He then broke into an appalling American *plume de ma tante* French, which was a piddling pastiche of the real thing. Before I spoke, I thought 'What am I to do if he wants me to play the part?' I didn't dare shake the faith of the possible provider of my future dinners, by topping him. I gently hinted I had made a French film for Paramount in Paris, but that fell on stony ground. His disappointment was obvious when I spoke my fluent French – it was nothing like his conception of it. Exit me!

Max Bygraves emptied a whole bag of confetti over the head of my lady friend (a journalist on *The People*) and myself as we sat in the front row of the stalls at the London Palladium. As Max and I hadn't met for quite a while, I wasn't sure whether he had taken on weight or just authority.

We had first met in Jersey, when Max was on a variety bill which I topped because of my popularity on radio with my series 'Waiting for Jane'. Our second meeting was when I appeared on Dorothy Ward's variety bill at Exeter and stayed on to compere a Sunday concert given by Cyril Stapleton and His Orchestra, supported by Max Bygraves and Robert Moreton, at the Odeon Cinema. In my introduction, I gave Max a tremendous build-up, as he was opening the next day for the first time at the Palladium.

Our third meeting was backstage after the show with my lady-journalist friend, plus the remains of the confetti Max had jokingly showered over us. We wanted a publicity story. As the stage-door keeper announced our arrival, we heard Max say 'I can only give Billy Milton a minute'. His dressing-room door was ajar and he spoke to me through the opening. When he became aware I was not alone he opened the door further and peered out. I then introduced 'My friend from *The People*'. Instantly his attitude changed. 'Do come in' he said pleasantly. Whereupon my friend drew herself up to her full five feet and said 'No thank you. Confetti is so difficult to get out of our hair and besides – we've had our minute!' She then swept out like a Rolls Royce that had just encountered a Mini.

When my fours years' contract with the United Hunts Club came to an end, because of their closing down, I received a phone call offering me the same salary for just three nights' work a week. I accepted without seeing the venue. That was a mistake. It was a place called 'The Club' situated close to the Hilton Hotel in Park Lane. It turned out to be a brothel.

On the opening night among the crazy quilt of humanity that were present, there were many who had obviously been born with sexual interests their parents hadn't bargained for. There were some over-liberated lovelies at my elbow and around my feet a few faggots – not the Joan of Arc type. I decided my opening was my closing, before the inevitable visitation of the boys in blue. There was one amusing high-light. Towards the end of the evening an elderly business executive arrived with a beautiful blonde, both were intoxicated. He was obviously delighted with his capture. The house-girls resented this newcomer, who was dressed in a low-cut white gown. I took in the scene, and when my eyes lighted on the big masculine feet in the white-satin slippers, I knew why they were angry.

Geraldo (famed Savoy Hotel bandleader, later agent) booked me at Cunard's 'London International', an engagement which lasted two years. It was a happy stint with amusing memories.

The miniature merry-go-round of hotel life is never without a laugh. Sometimes when I stop playing I cannot help overhearing tit-bits of conversations such as 'One more cocktail my dear, and I shall be under the host'.

On one occasion a lady asked a young girl, 'Griselda, how is your mother?' The girl replied brightly 'Oh, mummy's in bed with three nurses'.

'Do come and see me, my dear, when you have less time to spare.'

'Did she train to be rude, or does it come naturally?'

'She'll die of curvature of the bed.'

'She's such a social climber.' 'Really? Up or down, dear?'

Most evenings it is all splendour and feminine gender, enlivened by wealthy men with enormous amatory appetites accompanied by their ever-changing escorts. But there are times when playing is as much fun as walking through a plate-glass window. One aristocratic old crone in coffee lace and varicose veins as big as walnuts, was relentless with requests to a point of exhaustion. As her husband was dull to a point of genius, I expect she enjoyed taking it out on me. I was told she still had on her mantelshelf the invitation to a ball she received from Queen Victoria.

As a rule the Maître d'Hotel takes orders for dinner from guests as they sit in the cocktail lounge. One night he suggested to two newly-weds they take as a main course Coq au Vin – or Coq à l'anglaise. The wife shook her head and said smiling innocently 'No thank you. We have so much coq at home.'

I played for many private functions; some were fun, others rather tire-some. I remember playing requests for a dowager duchess for over an hour. I rose, intent on making a discreet exit. 'And where are you going?' demanded the martinet. 'To fix my veil' I replied. One lady came up to me, stared and said 'Billy Milton? Surely it was you who used to dance with Noël Coward?' 'Yes', I replied 'But only fox-trots'.

I became accustomed to the sight of the society hostesses welcoming their guests, dressed in diaphanous gowns, floating about like over-wrought sea-anemones and quivering like jellies in a high wind, in case their soirées should turn out to be unsuccessful. There was generally a sprinkling of diplomats who, like good jugglers, manage to keep four balls in the air without losing their own. The vivid mixture included tense tycoons, party politicians and voluptuous actresses who would colour the scene.

Playing many different establishments has its hazards. Some have appalling pianos. On one occasion I complained only to be told indignantly 'But, we've just had it painted'. As if a coat of paint was a cure for its ills!

Flying to Majorca to make some television commercials, I found film star George Sanders sitting beside me. I started to chat but he seemed withdrawn and reluctant to do so. At the airport I was met and whisked off to a new hotel where I was to be filmed testing mattresses, prior to the invasion of hordes of summer tourists. This I did with a sexy leer on my face whilst nodding approval. The next one was a close-up of the ecstasy I experienced as I tasted a sip of tomato soup. In reality it was tasteless. The chef had put in so much flour, you could have stood a spoon in it.

Not long after this, David Shaw, the financial wizard, who at that time was behind the Stigwood organisation, invited me to fly to Paris to attend the premiere of the concert edition of *Jesus Christ Superstar*, at the Palais de Chaillot Theatre. I was sitting peacefully in the third row of the dress circle, and during the interval I rose from my seat to walk along the gang-way of the front row to go to the toilet. A Gendarme intervened and without explanation, indicated I would have to make my way right up to the back of the circle to achieve my purpose. I was later told the reason. It appears that extra-heavy electrical equipment had been installed in the boxes that fronted the circle and this had made it unsafe. My mind boggled at the horrendous thought that the weight of my solid frame might have sent mountains of masonry cascading down on the heads of the Aga Khan, Salvador Dali and other world famous people sitting in the stalls.

Allan Warren (the photographer who was on an assignment to cover the event) and I were dining at the Lancaster Hotel, when he spotted George Sanders sitting behind me. I made the introductions which resulted

Playing Dr Crippen on television.

in a quick photographic session in Allan's suite. This strange sequence of events culminated the following week in Spain. George Sanders committed suicide. The world press clamoured to use Allan's last picture of this ill-fated film star. What makes the whole episode more poignant is the fact that Allan Warren makes a point of saying to each sitter – 'This is your last picture. How would you like it taken?' After a pause, George Sanders said 'Smiling'.

I played the piano for the party to launch Allan Warren's book *Nobs and Nosh*. As Lord Louis Mountbatten said 'Hello' to me, and Gloria Swanson, Evelyn Laye and other friends gathered round the piano, my mind sprang back to the concert I gave for Lord Louis' daughter Iris, at their Cheltenham home during the war.

Iris asked me to meet her at the Café de Paris in Coventry Street (the 'in' place for society in the 1940s) to discuss the programme. Ken 'Snake-Hips' Johnson, the young coloured bandleader whose orchestra was playing there, joined us later as he was to be one of the star attractions at the concert. This led to someone, who had observed us sitting together, sending next day a malicious anonymous letter to Lady Mountbatten saying 'It was a scandal that Iris should be seen in a public place hob-nobbing with theatricals and niggers'. The letter was signed 'A family friend'.

The concert was a success and a week later, 'Snake-Hips' Johnson and I were sitting together at the Embassy Club in Bond Street, where I was in cabaret. It was early in the evening and we were having a snack prior to starting our respective jobs, when a heavy air raid developed. Snake-Hips, like myself, was a stickler for punctuality, and he made a move to go. I begged him not to risk walking to the Café de Paris with all the flack falling, but it was useless, he would not listen. With the words 'I've never been late yet' he said 'Goodbye' and went to his death. As he walked on to the bandstand, the Café de Paris received a direct hit.

It was at the *Nobs and Nosh* party that I first met Liberace. The room was so crowded that when Allan, with his impish sense of humour, came up to me and said 'Would you play if you knew Liberace was standing behind you?' 'Certainly not!' I replied. The beaming face of Liberace then looked over my shoulder. I stopped, amazed. He warmly shook my hand and in so doing scratched it with his famous piano-shaped ring encrusted with diamonds. I found him most charming and very knowledgeable about our business. I remember him saying 'Billy, don't worry if everybody doesn't like you – just wait until they do!'

I played the piano at the party to launch *Nobs and Noshes*, a book by Allan

An episode of 'The Avengers' with Honor Blackman.
[ABC TELEVISION]

The owners of Cunard International Hotel (the Trafalgar House Group) have recently taken over the Ritz Hotel in Piccadilly, where in the 1930s, I played so many times in cabaret. That was the heyday of the great hotel. Everyone had suites with Dom Perignon on tap. We were permanently pixilated. For the Ascot gala nights there were hostesses like Chick Barnes, the piano heiress, and my very dear friend Lady Doverdale. I met her in the chorus of *Bitter Sweet* on Broadway when she was a pretty little Australian dancer called Audrey Pointing. 'Billy, darling' she'd say, 'the only thing I loathe at the Ritz is afternoon tea. That blasted fountain had me running to the loo for hours.'

One day I was threatened by a testy old peer that if I sang the number his wife had requested, he would black my eye. I sent for the manager and asked what I should do. He said 'If madam requests it take no notice of his lordship. She wears the trousers.' It was an amusing little ditty written by a bird fancier to his fiancée entitled 'I'm building a cage for your tits'.

My current engagement (at the moment of writing, I'm in my third year) is at the charming Chesterfield Hotel, off Berkeley Square. The general manager, Graham Tomlinson, aims at quiet elegance, first class service and good music. Realising the importance of the latter, he made sure when I first went there I had a new piano. To bring this lovely inanimate object to life, I have to cajole, stroke, strike and glide my fingers over its complicated anatomy when I entertain at the piano.

Every evening sees a fresh challenge, and I'm there to deliver an instant menu of music. Over the years I've become quite a judge of character, and often a face conjures up a tune in my mind. It's the subsequent expression on that face which seals my fate.

I have a repertoire of over 1,500 tunes and if a guest says 'May I hear . . .?', I'm there right away. It might be a theme from a television series, a number in the hit parade or one of those golden standards. Serene senility gets its chance too. I try to please all tastes. I play, almost non-stop for four-and-a-half hours, and if you say 'that's a *tour de force*', all I think is 'Thank God I'm not forced to tour!'

How to finish this book? The question reminds me of what Noël Coward said to a budding playwright – 'You must have a strong last-act curtain.' After a moment's pause, the youth replied 'I think muslin would be nice, don't you?'

But this is a Book. In my case, it's too late for sweets, and too early for flowers. Why don't I retire? Retirement to me is when you spend the whole afternoon deciding which television programme you are going to watch in the evening, so you will have something to talk about in the morning. In the meantime I carry on, hoping that when I reach the next corner, a pleasant surprise awaits me. It always has.

Seated at my beautiful piano in the Chesterfield Hotel.

[210]

Index